Harley-Davidson

Sportster Hop-Up
& Customizing Guide

Todd Zallaps

Published by:
Wolfgang Publications Inc.
P.O. Box 223
Stillwater, MN 55082
www.wolfpub.com

Legals

First published in 2014 by Wolfgang Publications Inc.,
P.O. Box 223, Stillwater MN 55082

The information in this book is true and complete to the best of our
knowledge. All recommendations are made without any guarantee
on the part of the author or publisher, who also disclaim any liabili-
ty incurred in connection with the use of this data or specific details.

We recognize that some words, model names and designations, for
example, mentioned herein are the property of the trademark holder.
We use them for identification purposes only. This is not an official
publication.

ISBN 13: 978-1-935828-95-2
Printed and bound in U.S.A.

H-D Sportster Hop-Up & Customizing Guide

Page 51

Page 104

Page 128

Acknowledgements

First of all, I'd like to thank my family and friends for putting up with nothing but motorcycle talk for the past year. Also, a huge thanks to Kyle and the rest of the folks over at Lowbrow Customs - you kept both projects moving along as smoothly as possible! Thanks to Dan and "Brawny" over at The Speed Merchant, Jeff at Church of Choppers, Jarrod at DP Customs, and David at Burly Brand for the great photos! Thanks to Minneapolis Oxygen and Discount Steel for the supplies, raw materials and sound advice. Thanks to Mike over at Pro-Custom Powder Coating (twice) for all the sandblasting and finish work. And lastly, thanks to all of the people both online and in real life who have shared their knowledge with me on all things Sportster-related!

From The Publisher

Authors are hard to find. And the good ones, those that start out with a good idea and actually have the skill and determination to follow it through to the end, are a very rare species. Thus I was pretty stoked when a friend told me about this bartender/Sportster fanatic he met in Minneapolis. When I emailed Todd the first time, he explained that though he hadn't written any complete books, he did edit a scientific journal on the side. Two or three emails later Todd and I pretty much had a deal. As you can see, Todd Zallaps is one of those really rare authors who can come up with a good idea, and follow it through to the very end - even when the publisher says, "I need more pics in Chapter Two and more photos for this Chapter Five." Congrats to Todd.

Timothy Remus

Introduction

When I first started building motorcycles, I didn't know a soul in the "industry.". I loved motorcycles, but didn't really know anybody that was involved in them. I guess I was always the kid that watched the "cool" guys ride by on their choppers, hoping to one day have one myself. When I finally leaped in and got my first real motorcycle (a 1964 Harley-Davidson Sportster XLCH), I realized that I didn't have any idea what I was doing. I'd read all sorts of magazines and books on motorcycles, but I had no "real world" hands-on experience. Most of the online resources that are available now were in their infancy back then, and very few of the publications were as in-depth (at a beginner level) as I'd hoped. Luckily I wasn't completely in the dark, as I had a father who worked for Ford Motor Company for many years that taught me the valuable lesson that if you take something apart- it can always be put back together. With that in my head, I completely disassembled and rebuilt the '64, hitting just about every snag you could imagine. Almost two years later, I finally got her running and immediately sold her to fund my next project. I think in the case of that motorcycle, I was too fed up with all of the problems I ran into combined with my inexperience to really enjoy what I'd built. With each new project, the more I learned- the more I actually enjoyed what I was doing. Eventually, it became my drive to try and make each Sportster I built a little better than the last.

When approached about writing a book about Sportster customization, I wanted to make sure that it was focused on the burgeoning garage builder. Along with that, I wanted to provide some history on the Sportster that would explain the origins of the motorcycle about which I am so enthusiastic. I wanted to produce builds that were a mix of bought and fabricated parts to show the many options that can produce an outstanding custom motorcycle. I wanted to show that "store-bought-custom" parts are often a fine complement to the fabrication projects you take on yourself- you have to take into consideration the cost-effectiveness of all of it. I wanted to present projects related to the builds that the average guy (and hopefully gal!) would not find too intimidating to take on themselves. And lastly, I wanted to assure the reader that help is out there- the resources we have as home builders are endless these days, both online and in written text. I hope to have done all of these things in the following pages. Most of all, I hope that you the reader understand that mistakes will be made- parts are going to get junked. The only way to learn is through trial and error. So get out there and turn that Sportster into something that sparks the imagination of the next generation of young builders!

Chapter One

Some Sportster History

Long Live the Sportster

To start out this chapter, I would like to present the disclaimer that I am in no way an expert on the Sportster. I have read as much information on the model as I have been able to, and have learned quite a bit about the particular models that interest me. I've certainly tried to be as accurate as possible in the following section, but I have left out many models that have appeared throughout the years. Basically the following is a rough history of the particular models that have interested me or influenced my builds. In reading this section, you'll probably find that my tastes lean towards the more stripped-down, race-worthy models that Harley-Davidson has produced.

1964 XLCH. The model that got me started. Mine never looked as nice as this.

Doug Mitchel

However, throughout the history of the model, the Sportster has seen iterations that included everything from retro café-styled cruisers to bare bones muscle bikes, to luggage-equipped tourers. That said, keep in mind that the Sportster is by far the most versatile model that Harley-Davidson has ever produced - which makes it a perfect platform for the custom builder.

The Sportster, as the world knows it, was born in 1957, and enjoys the longest production run in Harley-Davidson motorcycle history. Originally produced as an answer to the British bikes that flooded into the United States in the early 1950's, it was a drastic departure from previous models. Until the 1950's, Harley-Davidson's competition was mostly domestic, and was primarily limited to larger, heavier motorcycles. But with the introduction of the British models to American soil, there became a need to produce a model that was lighter, and more agile to keep up with new foreign offerings.

Backtracking a little bit, it could be said that the original K models were the first true "Sportster". In 1952, the K was the model introduced to compete with BSA, Norton, and Triumph. In many ways it was more of a hybrid than a truly original model, as it did share some aspects of previous models, while incorporating some new ideas to decrease weight and increase performance. For starters, the K used a swingarm frame in place of the hard tail that was present on previous HD models. This, along with the telescoping front fork provided the customer with a comfort level that was previously unavailable in the HD model line. It also served to improve performance over previous W-series motorcycles. The K model power-

plant combined crankcase and transmission in one single unit. This provided for weight savings, as well as created a more compact design. Unfortunately, the K model motorcycles were not enough to deter the influx of foreign motorcycles onto American soil. Though they were a step in the right direction, their performance just wasn't enough to keep up with the likes of the British bikes.

In 1957, the tides began to change with the introduction of the first Sportster (XL) model. Many of the design characteristics of the K model were refined, and the powerplant was updated with overhead valves, and displaced 55 cubic inches. The early Sportster acquired the name "Ironhead" due to having cast iron cylinder heads and rocker boxes rather than the alloy heads that were popular at the time. The swingarm frame and front forks remained largely unchanged from the days of the K model. In 1958, the Ironhead was stripped down somewhat, and engine compression was raised to make it a much more competitive machine. This model became known as the XLCH or "Competition Hot", and was built alongside the standard XL. The XLCH eventually became

A beautiful example of the first true year of the Sportster- the 1957 XL.

Doug Mitchel

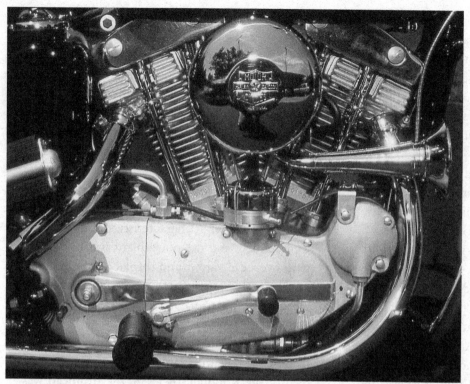

The 1957 engine. Note the cast iron rocker boxes and cylinder heads.

Doug Mitchel

the model of choice for many Sportster buyers. There were some minor engine/design enhancements and modifications between 1958 and 1969 including the electric start option in 1967, but for the most part the XL/XLCH denominations remained relatively true to form.

In 1969, Harley-Davidson was acquired by AMF (American Machine and Foundry). This began a period of production that many people consider to be of questionable quality. From everything I've heard and read, it didn't really effect the Sportster model until around 1972 - when the frame was changed from a cast-iron seat/shock connection area to stamped steel. The stamped steel section was not strong, and caused a need for a recall where the frames needed to be brought in to have a couple of steel bars welded in to provide additional strength. Beyond that, 1972 brought on the 61ci (1000cc) models, which gave the Sportster a needed boost in power.

Taking a step back a couple of years, I wanted to mention what I think are the two most important models in the formation of my love for the Sportster: the XR-750 and the XRTT. Though these two models were not built specifically for the street, they eventually influenced the direction of Sportsters to come. In 1969, the AMA (American Motorcyclist Association)

The 1970 XLH. This is the year of one of the builds in the book- it doesn't look anything like this one!

Doug Mitchel

8

rules were altered to allow for one displacement for dirt track racing of 750cc regardless of valve configuration. Previously, there had been differing displacement requirements for overhead-valve versus side-valve engines. Prior to 1969, there had been a maximum displacement of 500cc for overhead valve engines, and 750cc for side-valve engines. This rule was maintained primarily to keep the outdated American side-valve motors competitive on the track. With this change in rule, the previously dominant Harley-Davidson KR (flathead) models were now under direct attack from the British and Japanese. With the rule change in 1969, Harley-Davidson was forced to put together an OHV motorcycle that could compete with its foreign counterparts who had easily retrofitted to 650cc and shortly thereafter 750cc engines. The choice was made by Harley-Davidson engineers to use some of the existing architecture of the Sportster line to create a new dirt track racer. The XR-750 was born from the Ironhead roots of a married engine and transmission. The XR however had aluminum heads, a magneto versus a generator (which the XLCH shared), and a system of lubrication that differed slightly from the stock motors. Because the XR-750 was raced in AMA Class C, it was required that 200 of these motorcycles be available to purchase by the general public. They were special order however, and were priced beyond the reach of the average consumer. In competition, the XR is considered one of the most successful motorcycles of all time- with more wins in the AMA than any other motorcycle.

The XRTT, though built for road racing, was in the simplest terms an XR-750 with fairings. It did have a fiberglass fuel tank and fairing that were shaped for aerodynamics, along with an aluminum fuel tank for weight savings. The one major difference between the XRTT and the XR-750 was that the XRTT was actually supplied with brakes. The XR-750 dirt track racers did not come standard to the track with them, though the AMA did allow them. The XRTT came with a rear-disc, front-drum configuration, which was the last of its kind before racing motorcycles switched to all-around disc brakes. Aesthetically speaking, the 1972 XRTT is one of the most beautiful racing motorcycles ever produced. Its front fairing-to-tail balance is perfect, and the engine underneath is a beast.

1973 became the first year of full AMF production of the Sportster line. But until 1975, no major changes were made to the Sportster model. In 1975, the government mandated that the shifter be on the left side and that the brake pedal be on the right. AMF chose to not actually redesign the cases to accommodate the mandate, but rather spent two years producing models with a shaft spanning across the frame to relocate the shifter. In 1977, they finally redesigned the transmission case to accommodate a left-side shift. A lesser known model that appeared in 1977 was the fairly rare XLT 1000. Between 1977-78, right around 1100 of these "touring" models were pro-

The 1977 XR750. This is the model that started it all for me.

Doug Mitchel

9

duced for the general public. They had hard bags, a fairing, and the larger Superglide fuel tank. If you happen to see one of these online, let me know, as most people don't even know that they have one! Speaking of rare, 1977 was also the year of the "Confederate Edition". Because the 1976 "Liberty Edition" models sold so successfully in conjunction with America's bicentennial, some-body at Harley-Davidson thought following it up with a model that wore the rebel flag was a good idea. Apparently consumers didn't agree as less than 400 of the Sportster model were produced, making it one of the most rare of H-D models. 1977 also served as the year of birth for the XLCR - one of the most sought after collector models, and Harley-Davidson's attempt to sell a café racer. Unfortunately (or fortunately from a collector's standpoint), the model didn't sell as hoped, and it was discontinued in 1978 after only 3000 or so units were produced. The XLCR had minor frame

modifications that allowed for the removal of the oil pump while the engine was in the frame, as well as new brackets to allow for the mounting of the tail section. 1978 spelled the end of the XLCR, but it also gave us the 75th Anniversary trim package. The 1978 XL/XLH/XLCH models used the earlier style frames, which were switched over across the product line to the XLCR-style frames for the models produced from 1979-1981.

1979 brought some extensive changes to the Sportster line besides the move to the XLCR frame. The kick-start option officially ended with the 1979 model, however there were some 1980 and 1981 models that were released with kickers- most likely due to excessive factory stock. Disc brakes appeared front and rear, where previous models had drum rear brakes. Also, the exhaust on all models was dual-side rather than single-side-stacked on the motorcycle. The engine itself remained mostly unchanged cosmetically and

The 1977 XR750 engine. I love the dual carburetor setup. I plan to use it on a project in the very near future.

Doug Mitchel

mechanically, with the exception of the sprocket cover that made room for the rear master cylinder. Unfortunately, the changes to the 1979-81 models make them incompatible in many ways with other Ironhead models. Because the frame differed from previous models, the oil tank was redesigned to fit specifically in the rear triangle of the motorcycle. This oil tank is incompatible with other years. Rear shock location and fender mounting were also exclusive to those years, creating incompatibility with previous models.

1981 was the year of the repurchase of Harley-Davidson by a group of investors that included Willie G. Davidson, grandson of company co-founder William A. Davidson. An interesting side note is that Willie G. Davidson was also the designer of the 1977 XLCR café racer. To many, this was a sigh of relief that Harley-Davidson could return to its roots and continue building retro-cool motorcycles.

In 1983 the Sportster XR1000 was introduced to the consumer market. It was a long time coming for this model in terms of its heritage as it was based largely on the XR-750 from the early 1970's. The XR1000 was part street machine and part track bike, as it shared parts from the XLX as well as modified parts from the racing XR line. The XR1000 used two 36mm Dell'Orto carbs fitted with K&N filters from the factory, alloy heads with modified valves, and a dual exhaust that sat high off to the left side of the motorcycle. This package gave the XR1000 about 10 more horsepower than any of the available Sportster models at the time. Unfortunately, everything I've ever heard or read states that besides its noticeable power, and ability to stop due to upgraded disc brakes, the XR1000 was an extremely uncomfortable

machine to ride. Its suspension was soggy, and the weight of the exhaust caused a constant lean to one side. The engine itself was poorly balanced, and made for a shaky ride at higher RPMs. There were only about 1800 of the XR1000s produced between 1983-84, and because of their excessive price due to the machining and massaging required to fit parts, many of them went unsold until they were made available at a reduced price.

After many years of the Ironhead powerplant, 1986 saw the introduction of the Evolution engine. This is regarded by many as the end of an era, because the Ironhead is considered to be the last "true" Harley-Davidson powerplant. The first Evo Sportsters came in 883 and 1100cc configurations. With the exception of price, and cylinder bore, they were essentially the same engine. Both had aluminum cylinders and heads, which reduced weight and increased durability over previous Ironhead models. Cooling was improved over the Ironhead, as aluminum is a superior thermal conductor as compared to iron. Because both the blocks and the heads were aluminum, wear on gaskets was reduced, lowering issues with oil leakage. Overall, the Evolution engine probably saved Harley-Davidson from extinction. It proved that

The 1977 XLCR. One of the rarest of the Sportster models, its look provided for a "love it or hate it" relationship with consumers.

Doug Mitchel

an American company could produce a truly reliable engine that was at the same time powerful and efficient.

In an effort to attract a larger customer base, and at the 30th anniversary of the model itself, Harley-Davidson introduced the "hugger" model in 1987. The "hugger" brought the Sportster lower to the ground, by approximately 2.5 inches, to make it more readily accessible to shorter riders. I can assume that this was to attract more women to the motorcycle world, but Harley-Davidson never spent much time actually advertising towards that segment of the market. During this time however, the Sportster seemed to gain the reputation as a beginner's motorcycle because of its lighter weight and more compact size in comparison to Harley-Davidson's other offerings.

In 1988, the larger 1100cc model Sportster was upgraded to a 1200cc model. The carburetor was also upgraded to a Keihin Constant Velocity (CV) version. This change in carburetor made it easier to maintain good fuel efficiency while smoothing out the powerband effectively. The front end was improved with 39mm fork tubes to replace the previous 35mm versions. Cosmetically and mechanically, specific models did not change a whole lot in the next couple of years.

The next noteworthy changes in the Sportster line came between 1991 and 1993. In 1991, the previous 4-speed transmission was replaced with a smoother, more highway friendly 5-speed. Also that year, the higher end Sportster models received a belt drive as an upgrade from previous chain versions- the rest of the Sportster models followed suit in 1993. Design changes were made to the engine itself as well. The rear motor mount was integrated into the case, one piece pushrod covers were implemented, and the primary cover was redesigned. For the next 10 years or so, minor cosmetic and mechanical upgrades were made, but generally speaking the model did not have any major design changes until the early 2000's.

In 2004, the Sportster was redesigned with an all new frame that included a rubber-mounted engine to increase ride comfort. Also, the exhaust system was modified to hide the previously unsightly crossover pipe behind the mufflers. The oil tank was matched on the left side of the motorcycle with a cover for the battery. The transmission trap door was removed, which now necessitated a splitting of the cases to access the transmission.

Renewed interest by racing and sportbike fans came to Harley-Davidson with the release of the XR1200 in Europe in 2008. The XR1200 was a modern interpretation of the XR-750. It featured an inverted fork, a reworked motor, and XR-750-styled bodywork that included an integrated seat/tail section. The XR1200 also featured

The 1984 XR1000. The combination of street and track knowledge of its designers created a potent machine.

Doug Mitchel

fuel injection, which had become standard issue on all Sportsters in 2007. Unfortunately, the XR1200 was not released to the US market to coincide with the European release. The American consumer had to wait another year before they were finally able to pick one up at their dealership.

The XR1200 is my personal favorite as far as late-model Sportsters are concerned. It held true to the heritage of racing that the Sportster line possessed from the 1970s. It may not have had the performance to be a threat to other standard sportbikes, but it was a step in the right direction for the Sportster in my eyes. Harley-Davidson had dabbled in the sportbike market with Buell and MV Agusta, but beyond race-specific models, they never produced a "real" sportbike under their brand. Personally I've always hoped that Harley-Davidson would release a full-fairing late-model version of the XRTT in the Sportster line. How cool would it be to have an old-school Sportster

racer-styled motorcycle with brand new technology and safety sitting in your garage? But in recent years Harley-Davidson has preferred to create retro-remakes of other models. Maybe we will see one in the future, but it seems doubtful that they would ever take a departure that drastic from the standard models.

As this book is specific to customization for the homebuilder, I will forgo talking about more recent Sportster models. Not just because there haven't been a whole lot of major changes in recent years, but also because I wouldn't suspect that the homebuilder would take a brand new motorcycle and tear it apart for a major customization. Not that I'm saying you shouldn't do it- just that part of this book is about doing things that are cost-effective for the builder that doesn't have the resources to void the warranty on a Sportster to do major customization.

Today, the newest Sportster models have come full-circle. A combination of new technology and historic styling bring new life in the Sportster product line.

Harley-Davidson

13

Chapter Two

Planning the Sportster Project

Think First

The first step in planning a Sportster project is actually coming up with the proper model to work on. This may seem like an obvious part of the process, but various models have pros and cons. For instance, those of you out there who do not have the means to fabricate parts on your own might be better served buying a late-model Sportster - for which there are many aftermarket parts available. On the other hand, if you want something that will take lots of trial and error, will spend more time on a lift than on the road, and will take some sort of dark magic to actually get running - maybe an Ironhead is more your pace. I'm kidding of course, but the Sportster model

You can't just throw parts at a bike and expect it to turn into a cool custom. As illustrated here with this DP Customs bike, you need a theme - before you start buying and installing parts.

you pick can make a big difference in whether you actually get your project off the ground. The following paragraphs should give you a better idea of which model you should be looking for to begin your project.

THE PROS OF AN EVO

I would suggest that the person reading this book who wants to spend less time wrenching and more time riding would be better served with a later-model Evo Sportster. Now before the Ironhead guys stop reading this out of anger, let me explain this further! My major concern for the average rider is the safety of the motorcycle. I'm not saying that an Ironhead can't be a safe, dependable motorcycle. What I am saying is that if you are a fairly inexperienced mechanic, and run into a serious mechanical issue, the chances of finding somebody to help you out are much higher with a late-model motorcycle. These days you can't just take your Ironhead to the dealer for service. In fact, where I live I only know of a couple of shops that would touch my Ironhead if I threw up my hands and said, "I can't do this anymore - somebody else fix it!"(trust me, at some point you'll want to say it). That said, most shops that work on

All of these spare parts came on the Evo Project in this book. They will all be sold to fund this and future projects.

The Ironhead being customized in this book already had some interesting work done on it by a previous owner. Speed holes!

Sometimes it is better just to buy the whole lot of parts when you find something specific you need. The frame came cheap when I was looking for a front end.

Harley-Davidson motorcycles will service Evo-motored Sportsters. I realize that some dealerships put a year limit on the motorcycles they will service ("we won't work on anything pre-200X")- but even most of them will still deal with an Evo model.

Another upside to a late-model Sportster is that generally speaking, wear and tear will be much less on something that has been on the road for 10 years versus 40. I am not just talking about regular usage and environmental corrosion. I also include "home repair" in the idea of wear and tear. Consider how many owners might have done repairs on a 30+-year-old motorcycle. Then consider that it is very likely that at least a couple of those owners did repairs with the wrong tools (I'm talking about your "adjustable wrench"). Those incorrect tools mean stripped heads and threads that were most likely "repaired" by the same culprit. And those repairs generally were made using whatever nuts and bolts the owner could find around the garage. In most cases, a late-model Sporty wont have the mish mash of different nuts and bolts holding it together that an Ironhead might. I have purchased more than one Ironhead that cost me days of trying to sort out all the mixed hardware that previous owners had installed.

Price is going to be another factor that leans

Speed Merchant Sportster "The Exponent" – built by Brandon "Brawny" Holstein

toward the purchase of an Evo over an Ironhead. These days, you can pick up a running, used 883 (or in many cases a 1200) for the same price that is being asked for a running Ironhead. I've seen plenty of sub-$3k 883's for sale on Craigslist and eBay. With the price of a used Evo being so close to that of an Ironhead, it just makes good fiscal sense to buy the newer model. Also, if you shop for used Sportsters like I do, you can often find a reasonably priced model

Speed Merchant Sportster "The Mulato" – built by Brandon "Brawny" Holstein

that is loaded up with all sorts of chrome and touring equipment that you can turn around after the purchase and sell to finance your project.

Aftermarket parts availability is another plus to buying an Evo over an Ironhead. If you don't want to have to build a part yourself, your chances of finding something on the market for an Evo are much higher than they are for an Ironhead. I don't mean just aftermarket customization parts here (though those are easier to find for an Evo). I'm also taking into consideration the availability of new mechanical parts. In many cases, you will have the ability to find multiple manufacturers of a specific part for an Evo, where you might be hard-pressed to find a single manufacturer (that isn't backordered, or isn't a vendor for cheaply made foreign knock-offs) of certain parts for an Ironhead.

Frame detail work on Jeff Wright's 1999 Sportster.

A close up on the triple-tree detail of Jeff Wright's 1999 Sportster.

Interesting placement of an oil-cooler on Jeff Wright's 1999 Sportster.

THE PROS OF AN IRONHEAD

Some people are invariably going to say that there are no pros to owning an Ironhead. In fact there are literally thousands of failed Ironhead projects collecting dust in garages and yards throughout the country. That is the number one reason why they are a great project motorcycle! You can pick them up for a song under the right circumstances, and parts are readily available if you know where to look. Granted, those parts may be used, but in many cases they have many miles of use ahead of them. In fact, I got my start in this business by picking up Ironhead after Ironhead at swap meets mainly based on the need to have a certain part that would have cost me much more (and in many cases would have been inferior) from a foreign manufacturer than it actually cost to buy a basket case. Similar to what can be done with spare chrome etc. from an Evo purchase, I will often sell the parts I don't need from an Ironhead basket case to finance finishing my current project. There is always some other person out there that is looking for a part that you don't currently need!

Rarity is one of those areas where an Ironhead can win out over an Evo. Think of it this way, there are thousands of Evo Sportsters being driven out on the road. A running custom Ironhead is a much more rare thing to see indeed! Given the many years that have passed, and the number of Ironheads that were left to rot after breaking down - you are in a pretty select group of owners if you keep a well-maintained Ironhead in your garage! Consider that when you take your motorcycle down to the local Bike Night. There's going to be a bunch of guys there who are riding the same model (the Evo included), but you might be the only guy/girl there that is on 30+ year-old iron.

One thing I've learned in my years of ownership of both Evos and Ironheads is that owning a custom Ironhead forces you to have a truly "custom" motorcycle. As I mentioned previously, because of the scarcity of custom aftermarket parts you need to fabricate many of those parts yourself. I look at this as a positive. It is much easier to understand the intricacies of a motorcycle if you are actually building the parts for it yourself. Along with this comes pride of ownership. Its pretty cool to be able to say, "I built X myself" even if you are forced to do it because there are no aftermarket alternatives.

WHAT YEAR SHOULD I BUY

This is an interesting question, with no right answer. First of all, when it comes to Ironhead Sportsters, I generally look for pre-1970 models. I do this because I often change frames on these older models, and the VIN number was stamped

A 1972 Sportster tail section. I usually chop the tail on these frames due to the recall repair.

A Stormtrooper tail light lens from No School Choppers. A very cool addition to any project! Its all about the details!

on the engine case rather than the frame. It makes it much easier to deal with titling a custom motorcycle when you don't have to worry about whether or not the frame number matches the engine case number. In many cases, the frames have been modified with body filler, or have been smoothed down with a grinding wheel anyhow, so the frame VIN is long gone. I like the option of electric start, but can live without it depending on the model year (I can always go back and add a kick start to one of the early model electric start Ironheads). I stay away from the AMF recall frame models if I can, though if the deal is right I will take one and hardtail it to remove the weak seat/shock mount area. I like the extra power of the 1000cc models, but would generally stick to the 80's era versions for personal choice.

As far as Evo Sportsters go, I'm not as specific

This is one of the better show Sportsters I've seen in a while. I saw it at the Donnie Smith show in St. Paul. I neglected to get the name of the builder, but props for some great work!

about which model years I will or will not purchase. I prefer carbureted models for the simplicity of wiring, which means I prefer models pre-2007. I will generally look to purchase an 883 model over a 1200 because the conversion kits available are often cheaper than the premium you pay for a from-the-factory 1200. I like a rubber-mounted engine, but I don't like a transmission without a trap door- both of these things happened in 2004. I prefer the 5 speed transmission as well, so I look for post-1991 models. Other than that, it all comes down to factors related to condition of the motorcycle itself.

Even with my particular criteria for Ironheads and Evos, I still have a pretty wide range of both to choose from. And my opinion will certainly differ from yours in terms of which models fit the parameters you choose for a build. If you aren't going to take it too far from stock, it probably won't matter a whole lot which model you choose. But if you do plan to transform your Sportster dramatically, you will have to take into consideration the various pros and cons of each model.

YOU'VE FOUND YOUR SPORTSTER... NOW WHAT?

The first thing you need to decide is what type of theme your motorcycle is going to have. This doesn't necessarily mean that you have to plan for a wild one-off custom! Think of your

I try to keep two projects going at once when I can. It allows me to step away from one to work on another when I might hit a creative roadblock.

theme as a direction you would ultimately like your project to head. Just changing the handlebars on your motorcycle can change the theme of your project entirely! Do you want to build an old-school chopper with a stretched-out front end? Do you want to add a seat cowl and clubman bars and make a café-Sportster? Do you want to add aggressive tires, and some long travel shocks and make it a capable off-road machine? Figure that out, and you can begin to piece together some idea of what your "finished" project is going to be.

Get online and find some ideas you like! These days there are so many websites related to the customization of motorcycles, it shouldn't be hard to come up with some ideas you want to use for your own scoot. But the best advice I can give on the topic is - don't overdo it! The problem with so many of the home-built custom motorcycles I see these days is that they put too many ideas together that clutter up their project. Sure there are show bikes out there that are loaded with detail piece after detail piece, but at some point that begins to take away from the aesthetic beauty of the motorcycle. I've seen some pro-built bikes with intricate engraving, or insanely detailed metal work, but it's usually the simplicity of the rest of the bike that makes those details really pop.

Jesse Roche's 1974 Ironhead. One of my favorite builds with an amazing amount of detail.

Once you've come up with some solid ideas as to what you want to do with your motorcycle, you need to decide what parts you are going to buy, and what parts you are going to build yourself. If you are new to this, I would suggest there are some areas where you should strongly consider buying aftermarket over fabrication. I am all for building your own sheet metal components. However, if your welding experience is limited (or if you can't currently afford a

My 1970 Ironhead XLCH as I bought it. I rode it for some time in this form, but decided it was time for a change.

Speed Merchant's "The Mako". - built by Brandon "Brawny" Holstein. A great take on a modern café racer.

proper welder), it might be more trouble than it is worth to try and build a custom gas tank if you want to get out on the road quickly. You might find something that suits your needs in the pages of a catalog or online. Maybe a good compromise in this regard is to buy an after-market fuel tank and paint it yourself? That said, you only learn through experience. So find a swap meet or somebody online that has some crusty old tanks, get a cheap welder and get out there and try it.

As far as parts you purchase are concerned, you have lots of options! Go online and type in some keywords. You'll find resources for parts right away. The things to consider once you've found a few distributors are the actual price of the part, and shipping cost. I tend to keep my purchases to larger dollar amounts because many retailers offer free shipping once you've spent enough money. Other than that, person-to-person sale websites are another good option. However, they often limit you to a region, unless you are willing to drive a long way for a part (or trust the other person to actually send it to you after you've paid them - be careful!). Swap meets are another great resource for new and used parts. But keep in mind, they don't happen every week in most areas. So be sure to have a shopping list before you go.

The Bombshell, built by Yoichi Mori- an amazing custom that crosses the lines of a few different styles.

If you've got the tools (we will discuss this aspect later), and are going to fabricate some aspect of your motorcycle for yourself, find yourself a good source for materials. Trust me, you don't want to go buying sheet metal from the big box stores. They only sell limited sizes, and the markup is ridiculous. Find a supplier who sells by weight. They generally have a walk-thru showroom with all sorts of different sizes and materials. I make a weekly trip of heading down to my supplier. They give great advice on materials to use in certain circumstances, and have bin after bin of scrap pieces that can give me ideas for future projects!

Chopper Dave's Born Free 5 build The Steel Shoe. A street tracker that is ready for the track.

Once you've got some supplies, (and the tools to manipulate said supplies) its time to get started on the fabrication of your desired parts. The following chapters will give you some examples of projects you can undertake during your Sportster project.

SIMPLICITY IS THE NAME OF THE GAME

As was touched on in this chapter, simplicity often makes for a more aesthetically pleasing motorcycle. It can also serve another practical purpose when building a custom project. I'm a big proponent of the concept of shaving weight to increase speed and performance of a motorcycle. For instance, when I'm using a late-model Sportster for a project, I do everything

With just a few properly chosen accessories, you can create an amazing café racer. Burly Brand supplied the parts for this one.

Jeff Wright from Church of Choppers turned a 1999 Sportster into this work of art.

Jeff's use of detail work is amazing. I love "speed holes", and his Sportster displays no lack of them!

I can to reduce weight. This includes things like removing as much of the wiring as possible. Of course different laws will apply depending on where you live, but when I'm building a bike - blinkers, hand controls, and any wiring related to accessories I won't be using - get removed. Along with that, I will remove any excess parts that don't serve a practical (in my own eyes) purpose. It might seem like removing wiring might not reduce a whole lot of weight, but when you consider all of the extra parts and mounts that you remove in the process, it really adds up.

The simplification of the components on a motorcycle will make your life easier when it comes to repairs as well. Reducing the number of parts on a motorcycle means there are fewer things to worry about failing when you are on the road. I look at this as increasing the safety of the motorcycle. If I have less parts that can break, the better my odds are of avoiding a major catastrophe.

BRAKES

There are limits to this concept however. I know many builders these days are forgoing the front brake on custom builds - and though it can be aesthetically pleasing to see just the hub and some shiny spokes up front, I recommend against this as much as possible! Riding a motorcycle has inherent risks, why increase those risks (especially if you are an inexperienced rider) by taking away safety components that are proven to protect you. Of course you are going to build your project how you want to build it, and in most cases it wont ever be an issue (if you're careful), but you'll really want that front brake some day when the truck in front of you slams on its brakes and all you have is a underpowered rear drum brake to bring you to a halt!

THINGS TO LOOK FOR WHEN BUYING A USED SPORTSTER

When I'm shopping for a Sportster project, I have a very specific list of things I look for. I actually have a couple of checklists for both Ironheads and Evos that I take with me when I look at a potential motorcycle (most of these apply to a basket case as well!). I'm not going to give you everything I look for (I don't want you guys snapping up all the good used Sportsters before I get a chance), but I will give you some of the hints I use when I go out…

SAFETY FIRST

Check the frame carefully - are there any cracks at welds? Is there a large amount of Bondo anywhere (I learned this one the hard way - Bondo does not replace welding!)? Is a VIN apparent on later-model frame and does it match the title (early Ironheads were titled off the motor)? Check the swingarm for play as well as for wobble in the neck. Check the tires- are they old and cracked? Check

An engine detail shot of DP Customs' Defensor. That's about as clean as an Ironhead engine can get!

Alternately, the detail shot of Defensor 2, also by DP Customs. A more modern powerplant, but equally clean.

25

One of the cleanest late-model builds I've seen. Kyle over at Lowbrow Customs is the proud owner of this Gasbox-built, Angeldust-painted machine.

the sprockets and chain - are they excessively worn? Are the wheels dented or are spokes missing/damaged? Do the brakes feel soft; are the pads worn past safety? Are the hoses for fuel and oil in good shape, or are they cracked and discolored? What is the rust situation throughout the motorcycle? All these things can tell you about how the motorcycle was treated previously.

THE MOTOR

Check the fasteners (nuts/bolts/etc)- are they stripped out? Are there different sized bolts in places where there shouldn't be? Did they over-tighten and crack the primary, sprocket, or cam covers? Are any of the cooling fins cracked/missing? Does it leak any oil (this can be a relatively minor issue in some cases (especially on old Ironheads), but can mean major problems depending on where it is appearing. Check the engine cases, are there any cracks, or any welds that appear to have fixed major cracks? Bring a compression tester with you to check the compression of the cylinders (this mainly applies to a running motorcycle because ideally you want to do the test on a motor that is at operating temperature). On the Evo motorcycles, is it an 883 vs. a 1200? Finding an 883 is usually considerably cheaper, and you can hop it up to a 1250 for a pretty minor expense, less than the premium on the 1200 model.

The DiSalvo is DP Customs updated take on a classic style.

Bring a pencil along and check the oil tank. Is the oil ancient? Is there lots of sludge in the bottom of the tank? Pull the clutch, does it move smoothly? Does the clutch release?

Finally, the best thing you can do is take it for a test ride (after you do a pre-ride check of safety features of course). In the case of an Ironhead, if it runs smoothly and straight down the road and passes my visual inspection I'll usually at least be interested. I have enough parts on hand to make necessary minor repairs I might run into (then it all boils down to haggling). In terms of an Evo, it gets a little more complicated, due mainly to the systems themselves becoming more complicated. The road test will be the biggest influence on my decision as to whether or not to purchase the bike. Considering other factors such as accessories, features, mileage, and cost becomes a more involved process. Because there are so many more of the Evo Sportsters on the road, I have to scrutinize a used Evo model more than I might an Ironhead.

It's all about the details. Chris Edward's Ironhead makes use of wood in interesting ways.

Another example of Chris Edward's creative use of wood.

Chapter Three

Building a Café Evo Sportster

A Relatively Simple Transformation

I've found that there really isn't a good definition of what a "café racer" really is. Most would agree that it is usually a light and agile motorcycle, with low-slung handlebars and at least some sort of racing-style bodywork. It the 1960's when the term "café racer" was coined, it usually implied a European brand motorcycle. As time went on, Japanese motorcycles became the popular basis for café-style modifications. Harley-Davidson jumped on the bandwagon with the production XLCR in the late 1970's. I was never the biggest fan of the looks of that model, as many of the earlier British and Japanese versions looked much more aesthetically pleasing. My opinion aside, Harley proved that a café was plausible on an XL frame.

These days, many home builders are revisiting

The finished project, quite a change from the semi-stock bike seen on the facing page - nothing that you can't tackle at home.

28

the idea of a café racer. Because of this, my goal is to show that a café-style customization is a pretty simple thing to do with a late model Sportster. For the purposes of the following chapter, I'll be working with a 2002 Sportster 883 as a base for a mild café build. In the case of this particular motorcycle, the motor was punched up to a 1200 by the previous owner. With the exception of rewiring to minimize the electrical confusion, a more fitting intake, and a new exhaust, the engine itself will be left untouched.

The start of the café project is a 2002 Harley Davidson 883, punched out to a 1200, with a few pretty nice aftermarket parts on it already, some of them will be used on the "new" cafe racer.

SOME THINGS YOU NEED TO CONSIDER WHEN BUILDING A CAFÉ RACER.

When it comes to bodywork, you have a few options out there. You could choose to fabricate your own body panels from metal or fiberglass. Depending on the complexity of your bodywork, using metal will take some fairly advanced fabrication skills and tools or lots of patience. I'm not saying that the garage builder shouldn't take this path, just that the tools necessary to do a good job might not be cost-effective if you plan to do something complicated. Fiberglass on the other hand can be fairly inexpensive given you take the time to build prop-

The idea of turning this into a café racer actually started with a set of Biltwell Low Drag handlebars. I suppose technically using clip-on handlebars would provide more of a true cafe racer look, but for my personal use, I prefer the bars above my knees.

er foam molds, and are willing to deal with all of the mess. However, alternatively, you could purchase body parts from some of the many manufacturers out there today. Ryca Motors (rycamotors.com) produces a café racer kit as a package or component parts for late-model Sportsters. Burly Brand (burlybrand.com) produces café racer components including a tail section and café-style shocks. Roland Sands Design (rolandsands.com) is another manufacturer who has embraced the café styling and is producing a line of parts for Sportsters. All of them produce quality parts, and should be considered when entering the café-racer design stage. Keep in mind that as with any customization, bodywork is

In this case, I had intended to have the bars be a simple installation that implemented the use of all of the standard controls. However, once installed I found that the bars were hitting the tank. The simple fix would have been to add a spacer that would have raised the bars a fraction of an inch to clear the tank. The complicated fix was to begin taking off parts and reimagining the whole project.

The tank, seat, fenders, headlight, exhaust, and all wiring were removed to start this project. I usually thin out the wiring as much as possible. In this case, because I chose to remove the standard hand controls, removal of much of the wiring became necessary.

going to take varying levels of fabrication and fitment.

Some other companies to consider:
Storz Performance (storzperf.com)
Air-Tech Streamlining (airtech-streamlining.com)
Benjie's Café Racers (benjiescaferacer.com)
The Speed Merchant
(thespeedmerchant.bigcartel.com)

Once you have an idea of what you want to do with the bodywork of your Sportster, you can begin thinking about other aspects of the build that will give it a "café" feel. To me, that means removing as much weight as possible, bringing the handlebar position down, and fabricating compo-

nents that complement the look of a stripped down racer. For this particular project, I chose to address the exhaust, the suspension, and the aesthetics of the motor in conjunction with the bodywork to produce a modern interpretation of a café racer. Along with some fairly minor fabrication, a selection of aftermarket parts were used to bring the project together.

When I first started working on the Sportster I used for this build, I had intended to just throw on a thin two-up seat, some lower handlebars, and ride it as is. I had wanted something to ride while I was working on the Ironhead project. But once I got into the Ironhead, I decided that it would be

The first step in the process was to remove the triple tree to do a little customization of the front end. I wanted to have some retro components on this project, and figured some of Lowbrow Customs fork shrouds would be a good start.

These are how they come straight out of the box. A super easy install - just drop the fork legs and slide these into place. You can't use your front fender after you install these, but even if you could it would look weird to use both.

The finished installation of the fork shrouds. The headlight bucket I'll be using is black, along with the handlebars - so everything should look pretty cool when it is all buttoned up. At some point, I will turn down the fender mounts on the fork legs. But for now, I thought I'd leave them in case I decided I didn't like the look of the shrouds.

I'm using the stock front brake on this build, but I updated with stainless steel braided brake lines from Goodridge.

easier to bounce back and forth between the two projects since they were both going to get customized anyhow. It would have probably been faster to finish one and then the other, but I like to have lots of projects on my plate in case something gets frustrating and I need to walk away from it for a while.

I decided that the front end of the Evo needed to be cleaned up as much as possible. I began by removing all of the electrical components that I knew I wasn't going to need. This included the turn signals, housings for the switches on the handlebars, and all the extraneous wiring that ran to the rear of the motorcycle. Because only the headlight would be used on the front end, I didn't need to worry about saving much of the wiring loom. At this point, I went through and removed the rest of the wiring throughout the motorcycle. I try to take the loom out while keeping it as intact as possible for a couple of reasons. First, when it comes to wiring, I like to reuse the quick-disconnects that are stock to the wiring loom. So I will generally cut the wires a few inches back from the connectors and leave them in place to be soldered later. Second, because the wires are colored specific to a wiring diagram, I can splice wires with the same wiring color on other Sportster projects. I try to reuse as many parts as possible when I can.

Once the wiring was removed, I could begin making some changes to the front end that would suit my café

as well. The problem with the stock levers is mostly related to the unsightly space left when you use them without the switch pods. I'd already removed those, so I went ahead and used a set of the clutch and brake switch deletes from LC Fabrications. They just bolt on next to your levers and clean up the empty space nicely. Their price is right too in comparison to what it costs to get a new set

You can see both the Biltwell Whiskey throttle and the LC Fabrications Brake switch delete in this picture. They really cleaned up the controls on this build.

theme. The first thing I did was to remove the fork legs and install a set of the Lowbrow Customs fork shrouds. I had seen them online and had wanted to try a set of them for some time. Be aware that using these makes your front fender incompatible. I wasn't planning on using a front fender anyhow, so it didn't make much difference to me. I did leave the fender mounts untouched on the front end, just in case I wanted to go back and use them again (I didn't change my mind on this project). Installation was simple, and made for a cool retro-looking front end. Basically, you need to jack up the motorcycle to make sure you have enough height in your front end to lower the fork legs down from the triple trees. Then all you need to do is remove a few bolts that secure the fork legs to the triple trees, and slide the fork legs down so that you can install the fork shrouds. Once installed, slide the legs back up, bolt everything back down, and you are good to go.

Because the levers on the Sportster were in good shape, I wanted to reuse those on the project

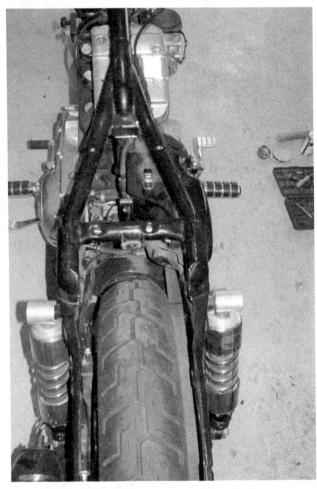

The rear of the project is going to be a little more involved than the front-end modification. For the sake of keeping costs down, I decided to build my own seat and tail section. There are options for doing this, but I decided to do something compact. I am changing up the shocks from those pictured, so that will raise the rear end quite a bit. I want the tail to stand out.

of levers. I also added a Biltwell Whiskey throttle to the controls for something more substantial than the standard housing. In order to tighten up the performance of the stock front brake, I also installed a braided stainless steel brake line from Goodridge. Once the front end was cleaned up, I was able to move on to some of the more substantial projects.

HAND-BUILT TAIL SECTION

I decided that I wanted to build a compact seat and tail section for the Evo project. This process can be as simple or as complicated as you decide to make it. I planned to keep my tail sec-

tion very simple, with space underneath to hide some of the electrical components that remain on the motorcycle. To begin, I generally build a mock-up out of manila folders and masking tape. Of course you can use whatever you have around the house, but these two items were readily available to me and provide a nice sturdy mock-up that is easily adjustable. I started by cutting out a very rough design that would approximate the footprint of the tail section. I made sure to mark any important points on the frame that might impact the fabrication of the component. Once I had my base laid out, I could begin to form the seat back

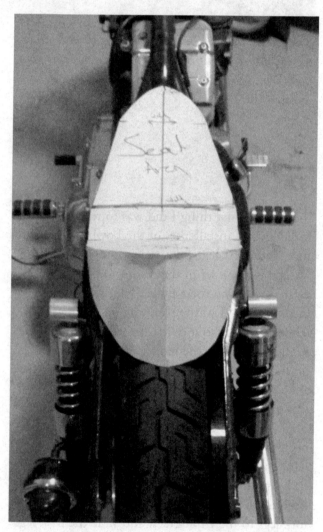

I began the project by taking a manila folder and laying out the shape of the frame. I marked any important points that would have an influence on the shape of the tail section. As you can see at this point, it is a very basic shape that just recognizes where the height of the frame changes.

I created a basic base shape that I liked in relation to the lines of the frame, then took another piece of folder and cut it into the shape I thought would work for the actual tail section. Next I taped the shape to the base material to form the model for the tail section.

and tail out of the folder material. Through a little trial and error, I came up with a basic shape for the tail, and taped everything together to form a three dimensional model that I would later transfer to sheet metal.

When it comes to laying out the mock-up form onto sheet metal, I simply needed to place the cardstock panels on the sheet and trace around it with a marker. I normally leave an extra ¼ to ½ inch around the outside of my traced panel to allow for adjustments as necessary. I then cut the separate pieces out of the sheet metal with

When it's all put together, I basically have two pieces of metal that need to be cut. I know now that based on the shape, there is a lot of frame material that needs to be removed from behind the shock mounts.

I need to clean up those fender mounts. Without them, and with so much open space behind the seat after they are removed, I'm going to have to come up with something that brings the rear end back together. With the shocks removed and the motorcycle jacked up to the proper height, I could get a better feel for work that needed to be done.

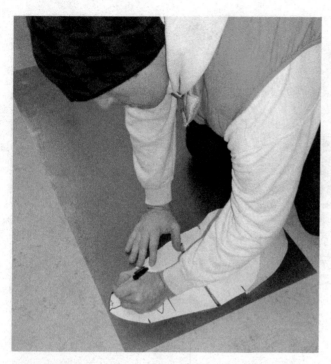

The folder model provided a basic shape for the sheet metal. My usual plan is to cut about a ¼ of an inch or so outside the model in order to make sure I can correct any issues in shape that might arise.

my cutting wheel and portable band saw. Because this was such a simplified tail section, I really only needed to cut out two major parts. The seat pan would need to be bent to create the back section that met the cowl. The cowl would need to be formed into an arc that was the same width as the distance between the frame rails.

Once my parts were all cut out of sheet metal, I needed to begin fitting them together. Based on my cardboard model, I knew that my seat pan would need a bend to meet the top of the cowl panel. Because I wanted a smooth bend, and not a sharp angle, all I really had to do was clamp the flat section down and bend it by hand. I used a piece of large c-channel I had laying around and clamped my seat pan to it. All I had to do then was secure the c-channel (which I did by standing on it), and bend the pan up around it. Once I had it bent to the angle that matched my mock-up, I could move on to forming the panel that would become the cowl.

The cowl section behind the seat was a little more complicated to form because it needed to be a nice round arc. If you've ever tried to manipulate steel, you know that it doesn't want to bend in a nice round arc. If you have the means, this is the time to use an English wheel to form the sheet metal that had been cut to form the cowl. If you don't, you have to come up with something a little more creative to get the shape you want. I have an English wheel, but decided to use a different technique to show that it isn't necessary equipment for a home builder. I looked around the shop and found a metal cylinder that was approximately the same diameter as the distance between the shock mounts on my frame. I found that the tanks on my oxy-acety-

The portable band saw provided the initial shape. As the picture shows, the initial shape is slightly oversized. I'll use the sander to clean up one edge of the sheet. Then I'll trace the finished edge to transfer over to the other side of the sheet to make sure that both sides are correct.

lene torch were close to the correct size, but I didn't want to be rolling those around for this project. I came up with a piece of heavy scrap metal tubing that was close to the size I needed and went to work. I took the cowl piece of sheet metal and clamped the flat edge that was going to eventually be welded to the seat back to the edge of the metal cylinder. Once secured, I rolled it back and forth on the edge of my workbench until I started to get a nice round bend.

Once I had a bend forming, I was able to remove the clamp and continue rolling until it was close to what I wanted. Once I was close, I could make adjustments on my knee that would meet the arc of the seat pan.

With the two major pieces formed, I could begin assembling the tail section. I got out the GMAW welder and tacked both pieces together at the center. I worked my way down the edge on both sides, tacking and making sure the arc of the cowl was lining up properly. Once I had both sides properly aligned and tacked, I went back and welded a small section at a time - moving around so that I didn't overheat and warp any of the metal. Once completed, I could address the side panel and round bar details I'd decided to include.

For the side panel, I wanted to use something fairly narrow that would provide support to the seat

After I get the initial seat pan shape correct, I work on the tail section. I cut the initial shape out based upon the paper model. Because of the gauge of steel, it wasn't the "bend over my knee" process I was hoping for. Instead, I took a piece of scrap tubing that fit between the fender rails and bent the plate using that as a guide. I made sure the edges of the tail fit the seat base and moved on to finishing.

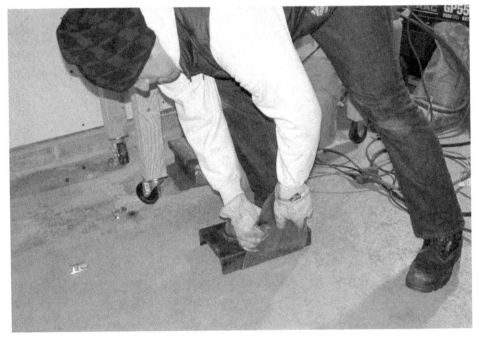

The seat base that I cut actually had the seat back thought out in the original shape. All I had to do was bend it into the correct position once the tail plate was correct. I scored the seat base with my grinder and used my weight and a large piece of c-channel to bend it to the angle I wanted.

I lined up the centerline of the seat base to the center-line of the tail curve and began tacking my way down the edges. Any gaps can be gently hammered down as you work your way down.

It took a little work, and I decided the angle of the seat back needed to be steeper, but the welds all came together quickly. I probably shouldn't have been welding on a wooden table, but I had a good connection and was basically spot welding my way down the edges of the tail section.

pan. I tacked a strip of flat stock that I had to the edge of the seat pan. With the same process I used to connect the cowl and seat pan, I tacked and bent my way around the base of the seat pan to form a support brace. I used my grinder to notch off the corner of the flat stock so that I could attach a detail piece that cleaned up the edge of the cowl. In the same way I bent the cowl arc, I bent a thin piece of bar stock to be welded around the edge of the cowl. I then tacked and welded the round bar to the edge of the cowl. I found the cen-terline of the seat pan and welded a mounting bung on the underside of the pan about two inches from the nose of the seat. I then measured away from the centerline on both sides of the seat back and welded on another couple of bungs for the rear seat mounts. Once all of the pieces were together, it was a matter of cleaning up all of the surfaces with the flap disc and wire wheel to prepare for powder coating.

As I'll discuss in the Ironhead chapter, I decided to send out all of my finishing work to the same company to save some money. And with this particular build, I wanted to keep the color scheme very simple because I was adding specific parts that I wanted to be the focus. I decided to match the tail section and tank powder coat to the same gloss black color of the frame.

To keep with the café racer theme, I decided that the rear shocks that were on the motorcy-cle when I bought it were not going to work. I enlisted the help of the guys over at Burly Brand for some of their Stiletto shocks. Unlike my other project, I wanted to raise the tail of my café to give it a more aggressive stance. Burly's shocks allow me to do this. Plus the red portion of the spring gave me an accent color I could use on other parts of the motorcycle. Before I could install the shocks however, I needed to remove the old rear fender mounts and fabricate a crossmember to bring together the look of the rear end.

After some deliberation, I cut off the fender mounts near a point I thought would look good after a little clean up. My band saw did the work here, though I could have used a cutting wheel just as well. Once removed, I cleaned up the area I'd cut off with my grinding wheel and flap discs. At the same time, I sanded off the area where I planned to install a crossmember to bring the frame together. For the crossmember, I decided on using some rectangular bar stock that I would bend to complement the arc of the rear tire. To create the proper bend, I went back and used the same cylinder that I'd used to bend the tail section pieces. I fired up the torch and heated the center of a long section of bar to be able to use leverage to bend it around the cylinder. Once I had the bend correct, I eyeballed the length of bar I'd need to use and marked it for cutting. Once again my band saw came in handy here, allowing me the ability to cut a clean line across the bar at an angle close to what I needed for proper welding. Once my crossmember was cut properly, I did some trial-and-error fitting of it

The initial welding all buttoned up. Because of the gauge of the steel , it wouldn't be strong enough on its own to be a proper seat. Also, I have a few wires and such I'd like to hide underneath it, so I will add a 1 inch piece of trim around the base of the seat. I could have rolled a bead along the back of the tail as well, but I thought it would look good to weld some small-diameter round bar around the edge of the tail.

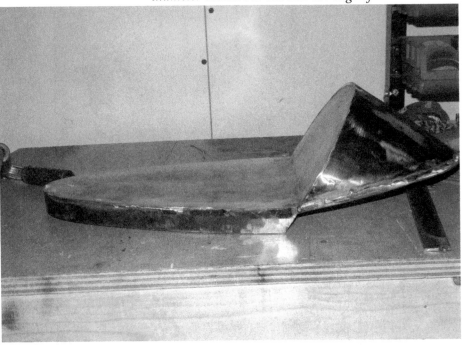

After the steel strip and round bar are installed, it's beginning to look a little more finished. At this point, the grinders come out to clean off the rest of the oxidization from the non-welded areas in preparation for powder coat.

IMG_0625 *Once finished, the seat is placed in its mount to check for fitment. I welded two mounts on the underside of the seat base that allowed me to use the previous seat mounting hole, and one on the new crossmember I will be building.*

Cutting off the fender mounts is pretty straightforward. I could have gone with a cutting wheel, but the band saw creates a lot less mess. Maybe I should have put the portable band saw on my list of must-have tools for the garage builder!

while cleaning it up with my grinder. Once it sat flush with the surface I'd prepared on the frame, I went ahead and laid down a root pass with my welder. In this case, I wasn't too concerned about the weld needing multiple passes for strength, but rather because I wanted to build up some welds on the front side of the crossmember so that I could grind down a smooth transition to the frame.

Once the crossmember was complete, I needed to attach the mounts for the rear of the seat. After tapping out the mounts I'd already attached to the seat prior to sending it out for powder coating, I mounted two bolts and tabs that would be welded to the crossmember. Because I roughly estimated where the crossmember was going to be in relation to the mounting bungs on my seat, I knew I might have to do some bending of the tabs to allow for the correct fit. I angled the tabs, bolted into the bungs in a position where I thought they looked best, and measured the distance away from the crossmember they were positioned at. I knew that was how much I would have to bend my tabs to make them fit correctly. I removed the tabs, and with my torch and a hammer and pliers bent them to the appropriate angle. I checked the tabs for fitment, cut them to length, and then welded them onto the crossmember.

Now that the crossmember was complete, I could go ahead and mount the shocks I'd mentioned earlier. They are a fairly simple bolt-on project, but you need to adjust them properly for efficient performance. The instructions provided with the shocks will fill you in on the proper method of adjustment. At some point, I would have to prime and paint the crossmember and the portion of the frame that I'd sanded down for welding, but for the time being I could continue assembly. Because the shocks are significantly longer than stock, Burly Brand mentions that there might be some exhaust bracket clearance issues with installation. This was the case with the installation on my project as well. It was minor, but the belt rubbed directly on the gusseted area of the exhaust bracket. Had I chosen to, I could have just clearanced the bracket somewhat and reused the original bracket. But because I intended to fabricate my own exhaust I just removed the bracket entirely. I would locate my exhaust bracket elsewhere once the exhaust was laid out.

Before I fabricated my exhaust, I had a couple of engine related projects I wanted to address. I'd already replaced the stock air cleaner on this project with a small Mooneyes round unit. Along with that, I installed a CV carburetor support bracket from TC Bros. Choppers, and a couple of breather bolts from Bench Mark. Also, because I had removed all of the controls on the handlebars, I needed to make some sort of arrangements for starting the motorcycle. I did this by installing a push-button directly on the starter solenoid. It's a very inexpensive part that is installed by removing 3 screws, and installing the manual button on the end of the housing. I suggest you make sure you are wearing gloves when you start your motorcycle after you install this part however, as this button puts your hands in a potentially hot place! The smaller size of the air cleaner

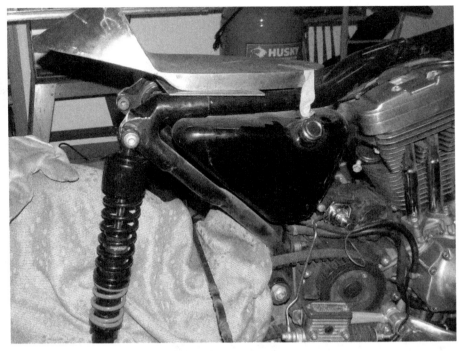

With the rear fender mounts removed, the shocks positioned where they should be, and the tail section placed in its proper location, we can check for any potential issues with the location of any of the components.

As this shot shows, some clean up of the area where the fender mounts were cut off is necessary. There is quite a bit of room under the seat for any electronics I choose to hide there. I do feel that there should be a crossmember fabricated to bring the two shock mounts together.

The rear fender mounts removed with the band saw. Now I need to address the cuts with my grinder and flap disc.

I broke out the torch and bent a piece of 1½ inch rectangular bar stock to connect the shock mounts. It took time with the grinder to mate the edges of the bar to the frame.

Upon looking for any issues due to the longer shocks, it became apparent that the rear exhaust mount was binding with the drive belt. I decided to build a new exhaust that didn't use the mount at all.

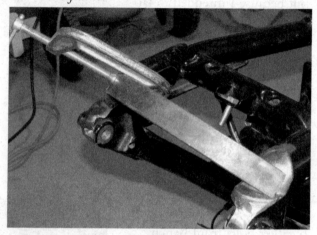

The piece is clamped and ready for welding. The surfaces mated flush, and after the initial root pass, I laid a few layering passes to be able to blend the welds appropriately to the frame.

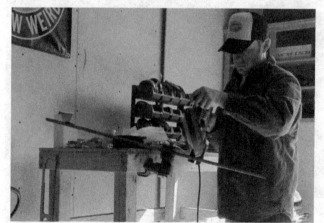

Cutting the bar stock for the frame connecting cross-member. My band saw gets lots of use.

The finished weld has fairly thick beads. I can use the grinder to clean up all of the excess. After masking I can paint the new piece without disassembly.

opened up the view of the engine somewhat, but I wanted to make more of the mechanicals visible if I could. Based on popular customizations I'd seen online and on other Sportsters on the road, I decided to modify both the cam cover and the sprocket cover.

CUTTING COVERS

To chop the cam cover is a fairly simple process that is only time consuming due to the finish grinding and sanding that needs to be done once the initial shape is formed. To remove the cover itself, you'll need to release a little pressure on the cams by loosening the rocker covers first. If you don't know how to do this, I suggest you check your service manual. It's a pretty simple process, and once you've done it you can remove the cam cover bolts and the cover should slide right off. I suggest giving the cam cover a tap or two with a rubber mallet to keep the cams in place while you slide the cover off. Once removed, you can begin the process of deciding how you want to trim your cam cover.

If you flip the cam cover over, you will notice that the area where the cam cover gasket sits makes a perfect outline for trimming off the excess part of the cover. I usually mark the area with a marker on the external side of the cam cover so I know where I am going to be cutting. There are a couple of things to consider before you start hacking at the cover. First of all, you have to consider that any cutting of the cover you do will be irreparable. Of course you can always buy another cam cover, but if you are going to attempt this project you need to make sure you are very careful with all the process. If you've decided that you are capable of this modification, you have to decide if you want to cut off the rear dowel pin support. I've chopped cam covers with and without removing the dowel pin support. I prefer the look of it chopped off, but it does provide alignment for the

The top view of the crossmember. Once cleaned up and painted, it should look pretty much like it belongs there. You can see the two bolt holes that will secure the tail section to the frame with quick-disconnects.

Given the travel of the rear wheel with the new shocks, I put an upward slope on the frame-connecting bar. I tried to match the slope of the wheel itself when I made the bend. I am always looking for angles or curves to match when I can.

Continued page 46

43

The Burly Brand Stiletto shock raises the rear end of the motorcycle quite a bit. It gives the Sportster a mean stance.

The Burly shock and the custom Stormtrooper tail light look pretty great together.

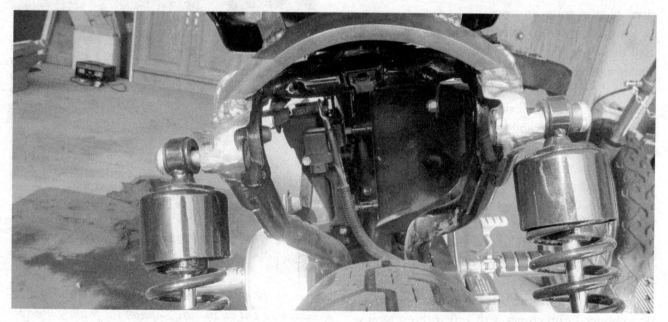

The view of the completed crossmember. It will need to be cleaned up and painted, but is otherwise ready to go.

I try to make motors on my projects look as "mechanical" as possible. Off come the cam and sprocket covers to get a little bit of customization.

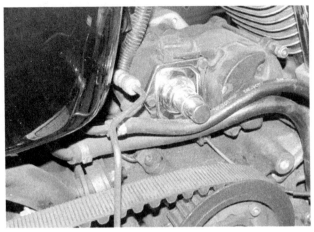

While I was at it (and since I removed all of the hand controls), I decided to install a plunger-style starter button. It bolts right on, and enables you to start the motorcycle without a handlebar switch.

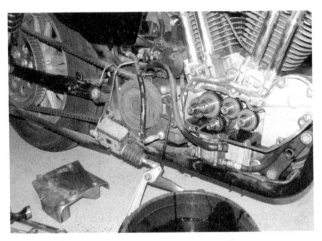

The cam cover and sprocket cover both removed. The outline of the cam cover gasket is visible here. That is the outline we will follow on the cam cover itself when we chop it down.

The sprocket cover has been removed for the chop treatment. Removing the cam cover can be a challenge without a manual - you will need to relieve the pressure on the pushrods by loosening the rocker boxes.

Looking at the sprocket cover, you can see that there is a lot of excess material towards the top. I am going to remove pretty much everything you see here, to expose the belt sprocket hidden behind.

Take care to keep track of your parts. This seems like a pretty simple process, but there are quite a few bolts involved. Be sure to check your manual for instructions. You have one of those right?

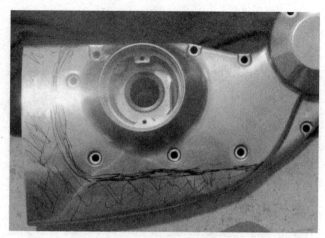

The removed cam cover with the material I plan to remove marked with sharpie. It follows some simple casting lines on the inside of the cover.

Once you remove all the excess material, you have some version of what is shown here. I took the sprocket cover down a bunch, and plan to remove the sprocket and paint it black.

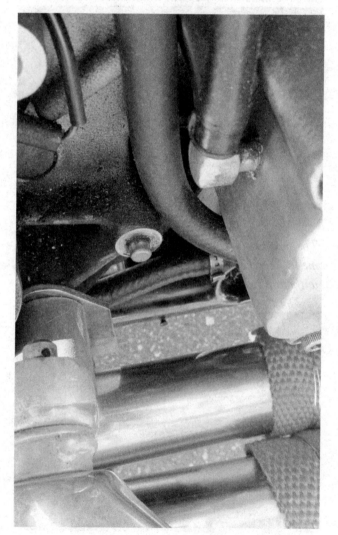

The dowel pin that centers the cam cover properly. You can decide whether or not you want to leave a provision for this on your chopped cam cover.

cam cover itself. I know plenty of people that remove it and have had no problems with their engines. On the other hand, it could be said that if you are planning on doing any performance upgrades within your engine (longer duration cams, etc.), then it might be safer to leave the support attached to your cam cover. In this case, I chose to remove the support, as I've never had problems either way.

Once you've outlined how much of the cover you want to remove, you have to figure out what you are going to use to remove the unwanted material. In my case, I usually take the band saw and make cuts in toward the gasket mounting area. I then cut off the excess material section by section, taking as much away with the band saw as possible. When I've come to the limits of my band saw, I switch to my grinder. It allows me to rough-in the more fluid shapes that are required to make a clean looking cover. After that, I switch to the flap discs on my grinder and surface conditioning discs on my die grinder to finish the process. If you have one of the chrome cam covers, you will either need to have the piece re-chromed or powder coated to finish the modification. As my cover had the "satin" finish, I was able to use the surface conditioning discs to blend the finish enough that the modification looked stock.

The sprocket cover takes a little bit more effort to remove, but gives you more options in

This is the completely finished cam cover, reinstalled with a new Biltwell Ripple ignition cover. Once the belt sprocket is painted, it will look like it belongs this way.

After measuring the tabs for the seat, I put a slight bend in them with my torch to properly meet the surface of the crossmember.

Once returned from powder coat, I mocked up the tank and tail section. I decided to use adhesive foam disks to mimic a racing seat. I will apply those when the build is complete.

I then proceeded to tack them into place with my Mig welder before removing the seat for the finish welds.

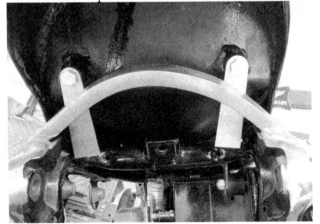

Because the mounting bungs were attached to the base of the seat before powdercoating, I have to create some tabs to mount the rear of the seat to the frame crossmember I added previously.

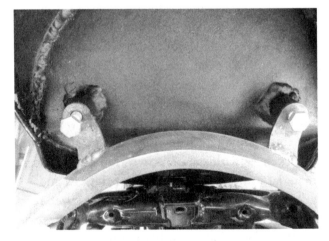

The tabs cut and welded onto the crossmember. Notice the slight bend that was worked into them so that they would fit appropriately.

These three mounts will be cut off and the frame repainted in this area to clean up this side of the motorcycle.

terms of how you can modify it in terms of the look you seek. To get to it on this project, I needed to take off the foot peg and rear master cylinder. Then I had to remove the bolts actually attaching the sprocket cover to the engine. Once removed, you have a lot of material to work with to modify the cover how you see fit. Many people drill holes or cut out specific sections of the cover itself. I recommend looking online to see if there is a sprocket cover modification you like and designing your own based on that. With mine, I decided to take as much of the cover off as possible. As with the cam cover, there were casting areas that could be followed to maintain the strength of the cover while removing most of it to expose the sprocket. As with the cam cover, removal of excess material was done by way of the band saw and grinder. Once cleaned up, the sprocket cover, rear master cylinder, and foot peg can all be returned to their proper locations. For the time being, I chose to leave the sprocket itself alone, though at some point I imagine I'll remove it and paint it black to cover up the unsightly rust.

ONE-OFF EXHAUST

The final project I wanted to complete on the Evo Café was the exhaust. I had recently picked up a Biltwell exhaust builders kit and decided that I'd break it out for this Sportster. The kit actually comes with the flanges for a few different models of Harley-Davidson, but I decided to cut the first few inches off of a set of stock exhaust pipes to begin the fabrication. I pick up stock Sportster exhausts at swap meets for this very reason. The flanges in the kits are on straight sections of pipe, and it can complicate the welding process to have to cut a couple of small turns to get good clearance off the cylinders. To me its just easier to cut up the stock pipe where the bends have already been made.

Once I have my initial flanges cut, I can begin the process of designing where I want my exhaust pipes to go. For this build, I wanted to bring the

The battery is the stock unit and still works well. As soon s it starts to get weak, I will build a more compact battery box or possibly add a provision for some tools behind the battery.

I got this roll of small round pads that I thought would make for a cool seat. I'm not sold on it quite yet, even though they seem to be pretty comfortable.

After the seat was securely mounted, I laid out the basic design of the neoprene "dots" for the seat.

The stick on pads placed in their final location. They seem to work in this photo, but I want to give them a good road test.

The Mooneyes air cleaner on the CV carburetor. Its compact and allows great visibility of the engine.

Bench Mark supplied these breather bolts. They are high-quality and look like they belong on the motor.

The other side of the engine. I don't love where the choke is located, and may move it to the other side of the engine. But for now, its original location will do.

I am going to make a custom exhaust for this build, and to begin I will start with an exhaust builders kit from Lowbrow Customs.

Even though the kit comes with Evo flanges, I decided to cut the flanges off an old exhaust because they have the tricky initial bend already in place.

rear pipe forward directly below the carburetor, then down towards the bottom frame rail just in front of the ignition cover. The front exhaust pipe would follow the frame rail down and terminate with the rear exhaust pipe just in front of the rear master cylinder, below the foot peg. Once I had an idea of where I wanted the pipes to go, I began the process of cutting bends and laying out each pipe. I've heard lots of different techniques for how to go about laying out the pipes. Some guys use welding wire to get an idea of their layout. Some people work from flange to tip or vice versa. I've always found it easiest to just cut some bends and position them near where I want them to go, and then take a marker to make "notes" as to how they are going to be tacked up. By "notes" I mean that I draw lines on the exhaust to show where I might need to cut out parts of the bend, or where they are properly aligned. Once I have a basic lay-out, I cut pieces down using my band saw and tack them with my GMAW welder directly on the motorcycle as I go. I keep a grinder close by in case I make a mistake, as well as to bevel pipe edges in preparation for welding.

Once I had the whole thing tacked together, I could pull the exhaust and finish weld everything. As with any thin-gauge material and GMAW welding, you need to be careful to move around, and do only a section at a time when you weld to prevent warpage. With pipes, this isn't usually a huge problem due to the odd shapes not allowing you to continue a weld for very long without addressing weld position. Once all of the welds were complete, I reinstalled the pipes and assessed placement of the exhaust mount. Because the pipes ran so close to the bottom frame rail and so close together, I needed to mount them from the bottom. I always look to use a mounting point that already exists on the motorcycle whenever possible. In this case, it happened that there was a mounting point located on the frame a couple of inches before the end of the pipes.

To make the rear mount for the pipes, I found the centerline in a strip of flat stock and drilled a series of holes that I would use to create a notch for a couple of bolts that would be welded to the bottom of my exhaust pipes. I bent the pipe in a

I am going to bring the rear exhaust back towards the front to keep the pipes near the same length, so I start by cutting a piece that is going to cross beneath the carburetor.

I've tacked sections of pipe onto the exhaust to bring the both of them to equal length under the footpegs. They run extremely tight to the frame, and shouldn't provide too much of a problem in a lean.

Here I've tacked a downward pipe onto the rear exhaust, and have tacked a section of the front exhaust that will hug the downtube at the front of the frame.

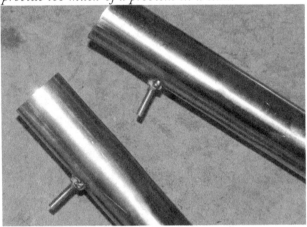

After the pipes are all tacked up and reading for welding, I removed them and installed a couple of bolts that I will cut down for mounting them to the frame.

Note, I've cut off the two tubes at matching points beneath the engine, and will proceed to cut them to length and create a solid mounting point.

Because it wont be seen beneath the pipes I fashioned a pretty basic mount for supporting the exhaust.

The exhaust is all welded up and mounted. All that remains now is to clean up the welds, and wrap the exhaust.

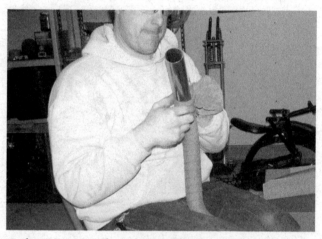

I chose to wrap the exhaust in red exhaust wrap to complement the café racer shocks. Be advised that exhaust wrap isn't much fun to work with, but given the right project, it can look really cool.

Work slow to keep the wrap as tight as possible. Some people recommend soaking the wrap in water first, but I decided to work dry. Keep the safety wire ready to keep things together.

90-degree angle, mocked it up in its position, and marked the two exhaust pipes for the bolts. I then welded a couple of short bolts to the bottom of the exhaust.

Because I knew I would be using exhaust wrap on this particular build, I didn't have to worry too much about what the pipes looked like underneath. I cleaned them up and smoothed out all the welds, but didn't focus too much time on blending everything as I would have if I'd been sending them in for chrome or ceramic coating. I found red exhaust wrap on a website and thought it would look pretty cool with the other red accents that I'd decided to use. I don't wrap exhausts very often, but with this build I thought it would complement the racer feel.

The hardest parts of wrapping an exhaust are the start and finish. When you begin, you need to make sure you secure the initial wraps with exhaust clamps or safety wire. In my case, I always have safety wire around, so I went with that. I've been told that if you soak the wrap in water before you start, the installation goes much smoother. I've tried it both ways and really haven't found much of a difference either way. I just throw on some leather gloves, and make sure I have spare clothes handy after struggling with it. When you start, be sure to fold the wrap over on itself a few inches so that the frayed edge doesn't stick out anywhere. Once you've gone around the pipe a time or two, use a clamp or safety wire to secure the first section in place. Then you can begin overlapping the wrap down the pipe leaving approximately ¼" to ½" of the previous wrap uncovered. Be aware that if you plan on leaving the wrap dry like I did, you will have to pull like crazy to keep the wrap tight. Be very careful that when you are stretching the wrap that it doesn't all turn on the pipe, otherwise you might as well start over. Because some of my angles were pretty extreme, it took a few efforts to get the wrap even and tight all the way to the end. Once finished, I safety-wired the end of the pipe and was all set to reinstall.

I didn't have a complete tear down with this project, so reassembly was fairly easy. The front end was cleaned up and assembled, and everything was checked for proper fit. The intake and exhaust were buttoned up and secured to their mounts. The tank was reattached in its stock position. The tail section was attached by way of a pin in front, and a couple of bolts in the rear. The rear suspension was dialed in and the belt was checked for proper clearance based on the new rear height. Wiring and hoses will be red to match the other accents on the project- with wiring greatly reduced due to the removal of many unnecessary electrical components. Most of the rest of the build came together fairly easily. There are always a few things I wish I would have addressed after a build ends, but I will leave those up to the next owner!

Once completed, I think the exhaust wrap complements the rear shocks nicely!

I added the decals from an old AMF tank to let people know I'm riding a Harley-Davidson. Plus it adds a cool detail to an otherwise plain tank.

Chapter Four

Evo Performance

A Little Too Much is Almost Enough

Much of the information I'll address later in the Ironhead Performance chapter can be applied to Evo Sportsters as well - especially those models with carburetors. However, with the increased level of technology of late-model Sportsters, there are some important performance enhancements that can be discussed that go beyond that of earlier models. As I'd discussed in the Ironhead performance chapter, there are essentially four areas

you need to consider when it comes to increased performance with your Sportster. Engine, intake, exhaust, and handling modifications must be addressed in some combination in order to maximize the abilities of your Sportster. The following chapter will give you some examples in each of those areas of enhancements that can be performed that will enable you to get the most out of your motorcycle.

The del Ray from DP is what a bare bones fast bike should look like! Great job.

ENGINE

Engine modifications on an Evo Sportster are much the same as they are for an Ironhead given that, in theory, the components of both engines are mechanically similar. Obviously, the "evolution" of the Sportster powertrain has allowed for such things as the use of aluminum over cast iron, or electronic fuel injection over carburetion. It should also be noted that the Evo powertrain also allows for the use of a wider range of performance parts based on a crankcase design that is superior to previous models. Freer flowing heads, larger pistons, and a longer stroke (though this is somewhat limited due to crankcase design) are all options when it comes to internal modifications for building power. Keep in mind however, that as with older Sportster models, it's a combination of the four "types" of modifications that really provide the operator with the most gains when it comes to power.

With engine modifications, you can follow the same rules for increasing the efficiency of dealing with the fuel-air mixture that you did with the Ironhead. Better flowing heads are the key first step in a well-rounded performance engine. With a modern Evo engine, sending your heads to a reputable shop is the best bet. A shop equipped with a 4-axis CNC machine and tested Evo Sportster-specific port designs is going to provide you with the most bang-for-the-buck. Reputable shops have machinists that understand the theory of engine design that the average home builder might not. If you don't understand concepts like "squish clearance" or "head decking", you should probably do a little research on engine design at the same time you are looking for a good shop. I'll discuss some of these shops a little later in this chapter, but it should be known that generally those shops that have Sportster-specific porting plans are also going to be able to provide a wide range of products and services related to Sportster performance. So check with them for recommendations based on your budget as to what your first performance steps should be.

When I look for a project Evo Sportster, I am almost always looking to find an 883 version.

A custom crankshaft from Hammer Performance. This one might as well be race ready!

Hotter cams can give you good power at a relatively low price. Be sure to get the correct cams for your purposes.

An XL Head goes under the knife in our proprietary 4-axis CNC porting process

The head porting process is one of the best first steps in building high performance.

An XR-1200 running a throaty exhaust, and remote-reservoir shocks. I'll bet that handles pretty well on the track.

More of a sleeper-type Sportster running the same type of exhaust. It looks pretty sedate, but I'll bet that Sportster could keep up with just about anybody.

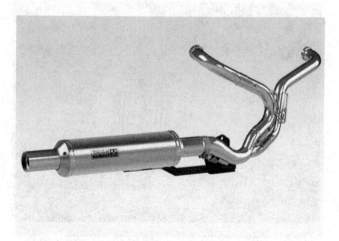

The Torquehammer exhaust. One of the best high-performance exhausts available.

Once and a while I find a good deal on a 1200, but the reality of it is that you can purchase and install a big-bore hop-up kit for an 883 from a reputable manufacturer for less than the premium you pay for a stock 1200. Also, the upgrade kits generally provide more power out of the box than the stock 1200 would. If you already have a 1200, all is not lost. You can upgrade all the way up to the neighborhood of 1700cc if you are willing to get your cases bored. But I'm getting a little ahead of myself here. Lets take a step back and discuss the 883 to 1200+ project first.

If you have an 883, and want to build power but don't want to completely disassemble your engine cases to have them bored oversize, the maximum displacement your stock cases will handle is right around 1250cc. The average big-bore kit on the market will basically be the same from every manufacturer in terms of components. However, quality of components and proprietary technology are going to differ significantly. I would suggest you not focus on finding a bargain as your primary means of selection when it comes to upgrading your bore size. First of all, do some research and find some performance shops that focus on Sportsters. A lot of times it seems that performance shops deal with Sportsters as an afterthought to expand their earning potential. You want to focus on a shop that places priority on Sportster performance, or at least gives it equal attention in comparison to big-twins. A couple that I can recommend that might not be on your radar are Hammer Performance and NRHS. Both of these shops are well respected in the Sportster-specific world, and have extensive experience in producing solid power with the Evo powerplant. Others, such as S&S and Zipper's might be a little more familiar to you in terms of industry popularity. But they also have spent lots of time optimizing performance on the modern Sportster powerplant. Either way, all of them produce quality parts, and have knowledgeable employees on staff that can help you with questions about your upgrade.

The standard big-bore kit from any of these manufacturers would normally consist of pistons

These are the workings of the standard big-bore kit. Pistons, cylinders and installation accessories are about all you need.

get off the production residue. You don't want any small pieces of metal scraping your new cylinder walls because you didn't clean them first. I suppose after you used some sort of degreaser, you could probably wash them in the dishwasher or something if you really wanted to get them clean. Just be careful though, your old lady might not care for that too much! After you have everything cleaned up (don't forget to clean all of

that have 10:1 compression in relation to your stock cylinder heads. Also, the kit would include new cylinders- which would either be cast-iron or iron-lined aluminum. Beyond that, you should normally receive all of the small parts related to the install of the cylinders and pistons, including rings, pins, gaskets etc. Every kit I've worked with has also come with extensive instructions as to the installation of the kit itself. I'm not going to spend a whole lot of time going over how the kit is actually installed, because most of the manufacturers have spent lots of time doing this for you with their kit instructions. If you follow them properly, and have the necessary tools on hand, there's no reason you shouldn't be able to tackle a standard big-bore kit in your home. However, there are a few things I would like to mention that you should consider when installing a big-bore kit on your own motorcycle.

First of all, after you receive your kit, clean your parts when you prep them for installation. I usually use brake cleaner or something like it to

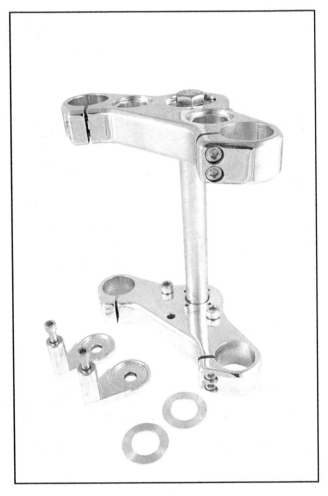

Even things like the type of triple trees you use can have a drastic effect on performance. If your motorcycle handles better, it can transfer more power to the road.

A powerful Brembo rear brake setup by DP Customs.

A high flow intake and exhaust make this Evo setup look pretty formidable.

the smaller parts as well), gapping your rings is probably the most important aspect of ensuring the proper performance and longevity of your new pistons. This can be done with careful measurement and a small hand file. Be sure that when you are filing the gap that you don't get it out of square or leave any burrs on it that will affect their performance. Take your time and do a good job here - your cylinder walls will last much longer if you do. Oh, and be sure to follow the instructions you receive with your kit in terms of placing which ring in which slot and which side is up as there are differences that will effect your motor if installed improperly.

The shocks my two projects started with. The short shocks are from the Evo project. It started out as a fairly low riding motorcycle. I fixed that by adding the extended café style shocks.

Don't skimp on tools when you are assembling a big-bore kit. A ring expander is a cheap tool, and without it you run the risk of scratching your piston. You've spent hundreds of dollars on the kit, what's $10 more? A ring gapping tool is more expensive, but still within the reach of the average home mechanic. I don't use one personally, but I bought precision files for gapping rings, so I might as well have paid a bit more for the specific tool.

Once you have your rings gapped and installed correctly on your pistons, it's a matter of installing them in the cylinders. If you see your service manual, you will find instructions on how to do this. I recom-

Replacing your cams isn't too bad if you're careful. I wasn't actually changing them out for this photo, but it gives a good view behind the cam cover.

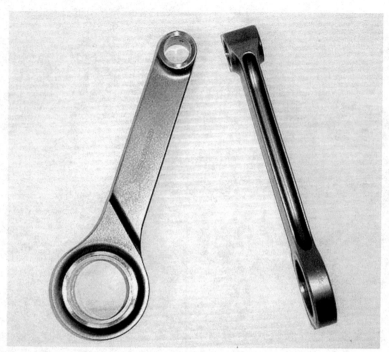

Connecting rods are an often over looked performance aspect. These from Carillo would probably hold up to racing!

mend using those instructions, but don't actually follow them myself. The manual essentially states that you should assemble the piston on the connecting rod before you place the cylinder over the whole mechanism (this is overly simplified, as specialty tools are used to align components for installation). I saw something years ago about a method of placing the piston in the cylinder first and then inserting the whole cylinder-piston mechanism over the connecting rod and onto the crankcase. This is the method I use when installing a big-bore kit. As far as the controversy over whether or not you should lube your pistons and cylinders, I always lubricate these parts on installation. To me, it can't hurt to do it, and will help to lessen any fear I might have about the rings fusing themselves to the piston during the break in period. Oh, and since I mentioned it, follow the break-in period instructions you receive with your kit. Don't just go out there and start testing your newly-found power right away. It will save you a lot of problems if you properly accustom your engine to changes in its internal environment.

AIR-FUEL

Once you've addressed porting your heads and/or installing a big-bore kit, the only way you are going to get the most out of them is to maximize the fuel-air mix coming in and the spent gasses going out. When it comes to fuel mixture, Evo Sportsters with carburetors are going to be tuned in much the same way older models were. You will need to find the proper jetting for your carburetor that allows for the most power with the least amount of wasted fuel.

If you are going to replace your cams, it might be a good idea to get adjustable pushrods and removable pushrod covers. It will make your life easier.

Depending on the brand of carburetor you are using, their websites will have base guidelines for what you should use for jets in a given situation. Beyond that, it will take some trial-and-error to find what is working for your particular engine combination. Like I mentioned earlier in this book, I don't think that there is one particular carburetor that is better than all the others. Each brand has positives and negatives that you will have to wade through to make a final decision on intake.

If you are working with a Sportster that has EFI, the format for maximizing performance is different, but the concepts are the same. Rather than physically changing out jets like you would on a carburetor, the EFI tuner makes adjustments via computer to parameters that effect fuel-air delivery. This tuning can be done by the home builder with the right equipment. Though in many cases to truly squeeze the most power out of what you have, it is a good idea to go to a performance shop that has a dyno to test your engine.

Mapping of an EFI is the standard process that a tuner would go through to maximize the areas of performance, fuel efficiency, and minimizing waste. To do this the most effectively, a tuner takes away as many conflicting variables as possible. That is to say that they want to test the engine in conditions where all other things are equal. This allows them to find the best combination of settings to maximize performance. Most companies that produce tuning equipment have spent a great deal of time gathering information on all of the potential combinations of commercially available intake and exhaust. Some even allow the tuner to enter a specific intake or exhaust model into the tuning system to give a good set of base parameters for further tuning. That's essentially the same thing as a carburetor company saying that you should use a specific jet size based on their testing to begin the tuning process.

IGNITION

The efficiency of EFI isn't just related to moving fuel into the cylinders by way of an elec-

Billet XL Intake Manifolds from HAMMER PERFORMANCE

Smoothing the passage into the cylinders helps to build power. These billet manifolds would help with that.

A good example of a free flowing aircleaner from Hammer Performance

Don't forget your suspension when thinking about performance. The fork adjusters shown here are from Speed Merchant, and they work wonders on the front end.

A high quality ignition system goes a long way in helping the performance of your motorcycle.

tronically monitored system. It also works in conjunction with an ignition system that converts the fuel-air mixture to explosive power. A proper ignition is key to efficiently burning the fuel-air mixture in your cylinders. In terms of a carbureted motorcycle, the ignition fires off a spark at a rate that is directly related to the timing of the motor. In the case of EFI, the ignition can be altered in such a way as to fluctuate based on determining factors to provide the most efficient burn in the engine. Because I use carbureted engines most frequently, I depend on ignitions that allow me to make parameter-changes in order to increase performance. Essentially the ignition allows me to set curves for how and when my spark is going to fire. EFI ignitions function in much the same way, but with the number of sensors involved in an EFI system, the process as a whole becomes more complicated. Because I don't deal with a whole lot of EFI bikes in my shop, I generally send tuning work out to the professionals. Much like a shop that does Sportster-specific performance machining, tuners usually have a very specific routine for figuring out base information that I might not be able to replicate as effectively in my own garage.

EXHAUST

When it comes to considering what type of

An 883 to 1200 big-bore kit from S&S. I've used S&S products for years and I've always been satisfied. You might pay a little bit more for the kit compared to other manufacturers, but you can be sure the quality will be top notch.

exhaust you should be using on your Evo Sportster, you need to base that on the type of intake you are using. Your choices for exhaust are going to be different for EFI than they would be with a carburetor-especially if your build will be maintaining all of the sensors located throughout an EFI system. If you are using a carbureted system, exhaust performance will mostly be based on finding a system that has the proper ratio of flow to backpressure for your particular needs. Even though I build most of my own exhausts, I have seen some really cool technology that would allow you to tune your exhaust in much the same way you would your intake. For instance, there are a few models of exhaust out there now that include a moveable valve that

Different pistons have different top configurations. This is mainly done to meet compression goals.

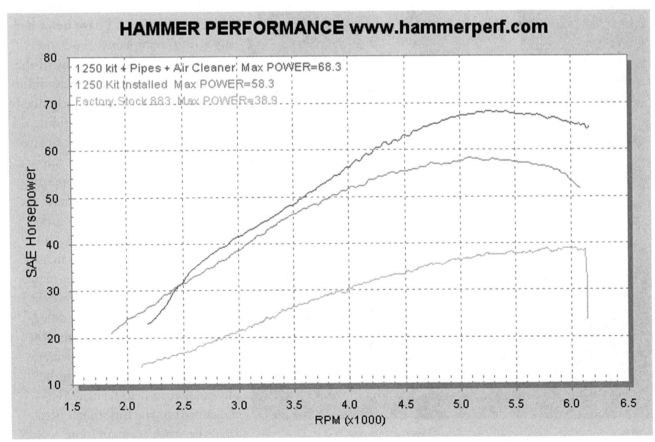

A dyno run showing the difference in power from the 883 to the 1250...Those are big gains!

can be turned to a fully-closed or fully-opened position (or anything in between) to provide power increases based on backpressure. The valve essentially either lets spent gasses flow directly through the pipe when fully open, or sends them through a muffler if fully closed. I like the concept of these exhausts in terms of their ability to be tuned for street or track. This type of exhaust also works effectively on an EFI model as well, but in either case to make a fully-open to fully-closed change in the valve position would likely necessitate remapping of the EFI or rejetting a carburetor. Either way, this exhaust could remain intact while changes were made.

Building an exhaust for an EFI Sportster is much the same as it is for any other model. The only difference is that you need to consider that an EFI system has oxygen sensors in the exhaust to monitor gasses. Many people just unplug the sensors and let the EFI control the fuel-air mixture without that parameter coming into play. Some build bungs into their fabrication process. With any EFI Sportster build I've done, I have left the oxygen sensors off. I can't say that it has had any negative effects on power. It probably makes a difference given all of the other factors involved, but being that I build street bikes, I can make up for the minor loss in performance in other places.

HANDLING

The last area you need to consider when it comes to building a performance-minded Evo Sportster is handling. When it comes to handling, Harley-Davidson has provided good-but-not-great systems for Sportsters for years. I have never had any serious complaints about the stock front suspension on any of the Sportsters I've owned. My reason for not complaining is more likely due to the fact that I'm so used to riding a specific way based upon stock components, that its as if I don't know any better. If you have the opportunity to ride a bunch of different motorcycles however, it becomes clear pretty quickly that there are some shortcomings to the standard Sportster forks. From a performance enhancement perspective however, there are a lot of companies doing things to tighten up weak areas in this component. Updated springs, and adjusters are available on the aftermarket to help regulate the movement of the fork much better than the stock configuration.

In the rear, there's an endless amount of suspension offerings to

Jeff Wright making copious use of speed holes on his Sportster.

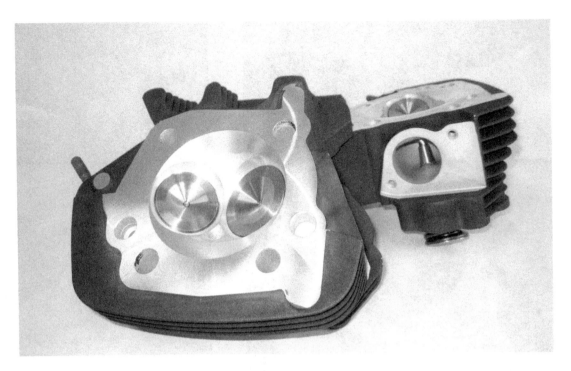

A set of reworked heads from NRHS - a good base for building high performance.

help better keep the power to the road. The lowering springs that were on my Evo project before I removed them were quality units that provided a smooth ride with a lower stance. Though the builds in this book were done in the dead of winter, the few test rides I have done with the shocks from Burly in the rear of the café project have shown them to be adjustable and comfortable.

The only real limit to your choice in terms of suspension is your budget. As I'd mentioned in the Ironhead chapter, sport bike forks are a fairly popular modification due to their superior performance. That is another option when it comes to Evo Sportsters. In many cases, only slight machining of your triple trees can give you all the performance benefits that the superbikes enjoy.

BRAKES

Stock brakes on late-model Sportsters are another "works well but not great" area of complaint for many owners. As with suspension options, brake options are equally numerous. I have never been so dissatisfied with the stock brakes on my daily rider Sportsters that I've felt the need to remove them for something else. Generally speaking, I will go ahead and switch out the brake lines for something a little stronger and that will provide the enhancement in perfor-

The correct gap in your rings is extremely important when building a performance engine. Here a ring is being ground down to the correct gap spec.

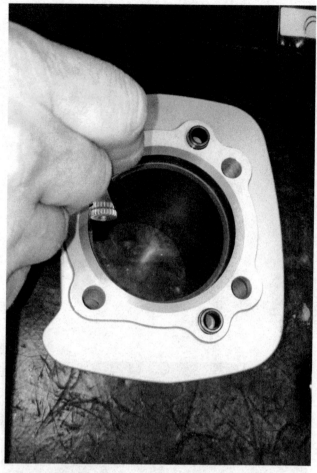

Check the gap of your rings individually in the cylinder. See your manual, or consult your performance shop, for the correct gap.

Specialized tools like this ring pliers are very helpful. It prevents damaging the rings or the piston on installation or removal of the rings.

A new NRHS cylinder being installed on a Sportster Evo motor.

mance that I need. But when it comes to custom builds, unique braking systems can make a huge difference in the look and performance of your build. Just as with front forks from sport bikes being a popular modification, brakes from those same models are also frequently used. In fact, there are a few different companies out there that are building adapters for specific brake calipers that have been known to perform well for Harley-Davidson forks. With a little machining or the proper adapters, the sky's the limit when it comes to high-performance braking and suspension.

Hopefully this chapter gave you a good basis for some of the performance enhancements available to Evo builders. With EFI things get a little more complicated than they would with a carbureted engine. The flipside of that coin is that there are plenty of programs out there that can help make the mapping process of EFI much more bearable. But if you are willing to accept the difference in how you go about making power between the two types of engines, you'll find that either one can produce a capable street machine.

An NRHS 1250 cylinder set up for honing - note the use of torque plates when honing.

The NRHS 1250 Evo kit as it comes from the manufacturer.

Chapter Five

Gallery

Exceptional Examples

There are at least a hundred different ways to customize and personalize your Sportster. Presented in this chapter are just a few that stand out for creativity and craftsmanship. Some, like the two from the Shadley Bros., are old skool cool. One is very traditional and could have been build in the '70s, while the other combines an older vibe with some modern touches and a few very unique features - like the one-off gas tanks.

A number of the bikes come from DP Customs: "It's just the two of us in our modest little shop and we like it that way," explains one of the two brothers. "No corporate b.s. to deal with and nobody to get in the way of our creativity.

DP Customs Café Racer. Note the Benelli tank, and matching hand-sculpted cowl.

DP Customs - "The Racer". I particularly like the coil-sprung seat setup and solid wheels on this model.

Another view of "The Racer". The simple paint scheme really brings out the mechanical details.

A too-fast stop caused the owner of the 1978 XL 1000 to park it in the shed behind the house - where it might still reside if it hadn't been rescued by Mark Shadley from Shadley Bros. As long as he had to repair the frame, Mark decided to stretch it 3 inches, while leaving the angle and height of the neck in the stock orientation.

Clip on bars are work of Mark's work. 39mm forks were trimmed on the lathe prior to installation - headlight and grille are from Headwinds.

Perhaps the piece de resistance, the twin tanks include one for gas and one for oil. Part of the gas tank includes a fabricated bulge that fits into a matching recess in the oil tank.

Extra attitude comes from the S&S carb mounted on a fabricated intake manifold and equipped with a color-matched velocity stack.

The old Ironhead came in for a complete rebuild before being reinstalled in the modified frame. Special touches include hidden oil lines that run "through" the fabricated battery box. Swingarm is 1-1/2 inches longer than stock. Rear frame extension wraps around and supports the seat, and also provides a place to mount the rear fender.

The very bright red paint is 4 coats of Hot Wheels Red from PPG sprayed over a silver base, with 4 coats of clear on top. Gold leaf and subtle pinstriping is the work of John Hartnett.

Another Ironhead from the Shadleys - one very sanitary XLCH circa 1966. The long list of subtle upgrades and customizing tricks starts at the front, where Mark modified a set of 39mm tubes and trees to work in the old Sporty frame, while keeping the drum brake.

Most of the hardware was retained, including the iconic XLCH cover, which had to be modified slightly to work with the larger diameter fork tubes.

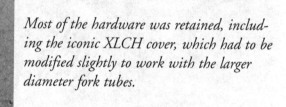

The Ironhead received a complete overhaul at the Shadley Bros. facility, including P+ cams and a complete valve job with hardened valve seats and stainless steel valves.

The gas tank with its "Sportster shape" is the stock item. Converting the 39mm tubes and trees meant the use of a new stem and neck bearings.

Stock taillight is welded to the fender and molded in place. Seat is a one-off item with a fabricated pan and a hand-tooled cover. Rear fender is from an FXR, and fit only after the struts were placed in a press and straightened out.

Built for Keith Lapides, "Black and Chrome" certainly lives up to its name - whatever isn't coated with black urethane and clear, sparkles with that shine that comes only from fresh triple-coated chrome plate.

DP Customs - "The Centennial". I like the tight upswept exhaust, and minimal rear cowl.

DP Customs - "Hollywood". Though blue and gold on this side, this motorcycle is red and gold on the other- a great paint idea.

Jeff Wright's Sportster. I could look at this motorcycle all day - there are so many amazing details.

Another view of Jeff's Sportster - it's a style all its own.

"Mele" by DP Customs - the pill-shaped oil tank fits nicely behind the engine.

"Mele"- The racing inspired rear fender is an interesting idea.

"Graffiti" by DP Customs - I love the racing inspired rear drag slick and exhaust.

Another view of "Graffiti" - looks ready for the track!

Chapter Six

The Ironhead Build

Not Quite a Chopper

I chose a 1970 Harley-Davidson XLCH as the basis for the Ironhead build that follows. This particular motorcycle has been a semi-daily rider for me for the last couple of years. Most of the original modifications were done by the previous owner, and I was riding it "as is" while I worked on other projects. I decided it was time to freshen it up a bit, as well as to use it as a testing model for some of the products available to Ironhead enthusiasts these days. I chose to make it a sort of

The finished bike from the "bad" side. Photographers shy away from this side of a motorcycle, but I think all the fins look great!

chopper hybrid- with a hardtail, but also with a standard rake front end so that it remained maneuverable on city streets.

I first did some research on the various methods of removing the rear suspension on the Ironhead frame. Basically you have a few options when deciding how to tackle this issue. You can either buy a new frame that already has a rear triangle welded on, buy a bolt-on/weld-on hardtail, or use struts to replace the standard shocks. Although struts are the cheapest method of creating a hardtail, it isn't really anything more than taking away the shocks and replacing them with solid metal bars. Aesthetically, I am not a big fan of struts. I would rather just switch to some covered shocks or find some spring struts than use a clumsy looking shock eye-to-eye connector. They don't do a great deal to lighten the frame either, because all of the swingarm hardware remains intact, and the strut is not much lighter than a shock.

Alternatively, you could choose to purchase an entirely new frame for your project. The downside to this method is the price. Most new frames come it at a price right around a thousand dollars. That can be too much to afford for the aspiring home-builder. If you have

This is the 1970 Ironhead as it started out. A few cool modifications, but with a sprung-rear end that I wanted to remove.

The beginnings of the rear end removal. I wasn't too worried about the wiring because I plan to move the regulator and simplify the wiring in general. The seat, rear fender, and shocks are removed - ready for the removal of the rear tire.

This mess all has to go! I am switching up to a generator-mounted regulator from Cycle Electric, all of this excess wiring can be removed. I'm going to hide the wiring and run lines through the frame.

The top view of the rear of the stock Ironhead frame. You can see that I've marked the area that will need to be removed in soapstone. Luckily I had a portable band saw for this job, but a grinder and some cutting wheels will do the job too.

Everything is removed in prep for the conversion. This particular hardtail involves removal of the cast shock-mount area. Some of the lower-cost conversions retain this section so you can return to a suspension.

This is the David Bird Ironhead conversion as it comes from the manufacturer. The welds are flawless, and the fitment is as it should be.

Once you have everything cut down, you should clean it up a little bit. This was before I cut off that remaining mount and angled the two downtubes to accept the Bird hardtail.

Here is the first fitment of the hardtail. Unlike many of the other hard tail conversions out there, this one creates a pretty good line down the backbone.

The hardtail attaches at the top of the frame using 2 bolts, 4 at the bottom. The original frame section has been ground down to accept the kit.

You will need to step-drill the top hole in relation to the bottom in order for the supplied sleeves to fit appropriately.

This is the bottom mounting point of the frame. As I need a new place for my battery box, I plan to use a couple of those bolt holes as a place to mount my battery box.

Once you've drilled your 2 top mounting holes, it's all pretty easy from there. It's a good idea to check everything for alignment at this point. From here, we have to figure out the placement of a few accessories.

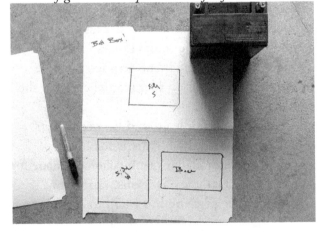

I use manila folders all the time. In this case, I traced around the battery, the outlines will be my template to cut out the panels for the battery box.

One of my many grinders makes an appearance in this photo. I've taken a sheet of steel that I'm going to fabricate my battery box out of, and laid out the appropriate cutting lines.

the money, this is the route that I would recommend however, as the lines of the frame will be clean, and the integrity of the frame itself- given proper welds and geometry- is the highest. This method allows for the most choices in tire size changes as well, as the frame geometry can be adjusted to allow for a wider rear wheel than the alternatives.

The logical middle ground between struts and a complete hardtail frame is the bolt-on/weld-on hardtail. This is the choice I made for my build for a couple of reasons. First, I was trying to keep the price on this build to a minimum for the sake of the audience - without using struts. Secondly, the particular model of bolt-on hardtail I chose to use is the first one I've seen

that maintains the lines of the frame the way I prefer. Most of the tail sections available for Ironhead frames have a very steep drop in the rear triangle due to being connected by bolts at the shock mount area. I never cared for this look, and hoped that eventually somebody would solve the geometry problem with a new design. David Bird accomplished this with his version of the bolt-on hardtail.

Because of Bird's design, you will have to do quite a bit more altering of the frame than you would if you just bought the types that bolt to the shock mount area. After removing the rear fender, seat, wheel and swingarm, you will need to grind down the rear of the frame to accept the hardtail. If you ever want to return to a rear-suspension, this particular type of hard-tail conversion is not for you. The instructions that come with the hardtail conversion tell you how to remove the proper amount of material to ensure proper fitment. Be aware that on the particular year-range that I was using, you have to grind the frame down at an angle so that the hardtail fits correctly. Its pretty straightforward, you may just have to check fitment and readjust a couple of times. Once I had the correct angles taken care of in grinding down the frame, I cleaned up any

I've welded the bulk of the box together. This would have been the place to show the method of scoring the metal with the grinder - the poor-man's brake. Because the box was small, I chose to weld both corners instead.

82

other spots that I could visibly fix before moving on.

While I had the grinder going to clean up the frame, I decided to remove some excess material from other parts of the Ironhead. I started with the front fork. This is a pretty common customization on hydraulic front forks these days. In many cases, builders will completely remove all the mounts on the fork legs and run a spool wheel in front. I don't like to be without a front brake, so I decided to just take down the fender and reflector mounts. The easiest way to accomplish this is to throw the fork legs on a lathe and take down any unwanted

You can see my box, and the grid - the guide for my lightening holes.

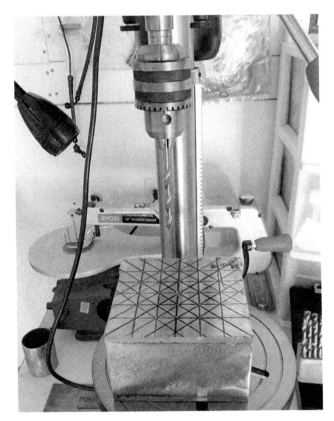

I chose to start from the center and work towards the edges. For safety, this piece should be clamped down-and be sure to drill pilot holes to save time.

The finished product: simple, but hugs the battery nicely. Mounting behind the motor is the next step.

This is how I want the battery box to fit. I placed the oil tank and rear fender in the picture to give myself some idea of fitments. The fender is in need of some radius work.

Cutting the fender blank down for the rear fender.

The frame flipped over with the mounts all welded into place. Be sure to double-check all your tacks as you go along. Otherwise you might be doing lots of extra grinding and welding to get your fitment correct.

I've reinstalled the rear wheel, I need to figure out a way to mount the seat, rear fender, and oil tank. I originally intended to fab up a small sissy bar but decided to go another route.

This is my preferred location for the seat, fender, and oil tank. Well maybe not so much the seat, as the slight downward angle of the rear section presents a minor problem as I am planning to hard mount the Biltwell solo seat.

material. But since I'm doing this without a lathe in my shop, I'm going to work them down with my cutting wheel and grinder, and then work my way down to finer sanding and finishing discs until I reach the finish I'm looking for. Be sure to take it slow. You can easily take too much off and cause a wave in the lines of your fork leg if you aren't careful. Once they are cleaned up to your liking, you can leave them as is, polish them, or have them chromed. I don't like shiny parts, so I am just going to finish them with a very fine abrasive pad and call them done. I can always go back and polish them if I choose.

At the same time as I was cleaning up the fork legs, I decided to address the cam cover, and the rocker boxes. I removed both so that I could have the highest amount of access to them and finished them the same way I had done the fork legs. I used a die grinder with 2-3" finishing discs for this procedure. If you go this route, be sure to keep the die grinder positioned at the same angle to the work throughout the process. This isn't of great importance if you are going to polish, because you can buff out swirl marks. But if you are stopping at the point of finishing discs, you will reduce unsightly uneven swirl marks if you keep things consistent. A tip: if you want to get very artistic, you can try putting a piece of dowel

Continued page 89

The battery box - with a couple of mounts tacked on. Mounts will fit between the 2 bolts on the bottom of the frame. Next I need to fab up another mount to connect the back of the box to the hardtail crossmember.

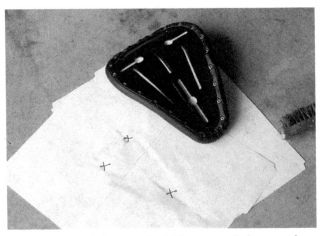

Another use of the manila folder. I needed a template to show where the mounting slots are located. I just took folder material and pressed it to the bottom of the seat to find the three bolt-insert holes.

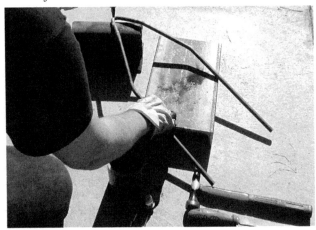

The round bar was partially bent for use as a sissy bar. With a torch I was able to reheat it and create bends more appropriate to its new use as a seat mount.

With the beginning angle correct, I clamped it to a work surface to create the slight upward bend for the back seat mounts. Then I could create the final bend that would continue to my fender bungs.

With the bends related to the seat mount made, a mounting point for the front of the subframe is necessary to align everything and to allow us to figure out the bends for the rear fender.

To properly position the rear fender in terms of distance from the wheel, I taped a couple of pieces of tubing to the wheel and aligned my fender on top of them.

After the mount was attached to the frame I created the initial bend that would allow me to mount the fender. Note that I used a piece of chain in place of the tubing as a spacer.

The underside of what will become the subframe with the thru-frame bolt installed. I decided to weld a small plate on the underside of the subframe as well to give the mounting point some strength.

I matched the angle of the round bar with the top of the rear triangle. It took work with the torch to make sure that both sides of the fender mounts were the same. This became more critical because I couldn't mount the fender to the frame in a third location. I welded 2 mounting bungs on the fender, and 2 on the ends of the fender mounting bars to accept 2 Allen head bolts.

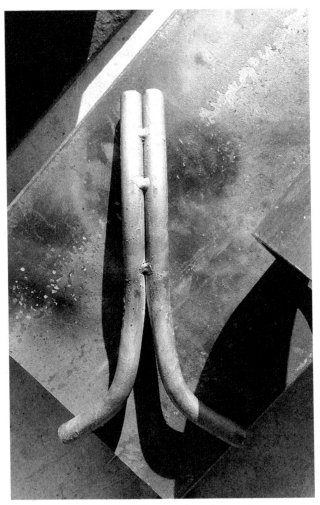

In order to keep the organic feel of the torch-bent steel of the seat/fender mount, I decided to fab an oil tank mount with some compound bends. I proceeded to weld two pieces of bar stock to my worktable, and used the torch to put a total of 3 bends into each bar.

I don't use the torch for welding often but, decided it would be appropriate here. I centered the oil tank mount between the two fender mount rails, and used the torch to weld the mount at an angle.

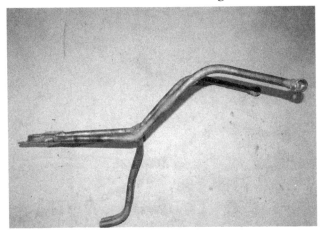

Here's the subframe with the front frame mount, the two fender mounts, and the oil tank mount coming together. I think it adds a really cool detail piece to this particular motorcycle.

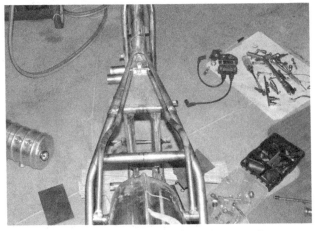

Here is the top view of the fender mounting bars, you can see that the seat, rear frame section, and fender all came into play when addressing the fabrication of the subframe. Now we move on to the oil tank.

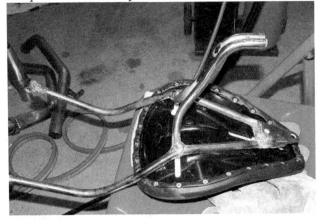

With the subframe removed, I was able to figure exactly where the seat mounts were going to be in terms of my tank mount. The seat's mounting bungs fit neatly between the bends of both, and were easily tacked in place without much effort.

The subframe installed - you can see the plate for the oil tank, the seat mounts and how the fender rails follow the lines of the rear triangle.

It's time to clean up some of the mounts. The risers are going to go too, Some of the electronics were originally held within the headlight, but the switch to a generator-mounted regulator, simplifies the wiring greatly.

I've cleaned up the top tree by removing unnecessary mounts and smoothing casting marks. I've decided to switch back to the H-D stock bottom tree which I'll clean up to match the top tree.

The legs can either be sanded down, or you can take off the major bits with a saw and then sand it down. If you have access, a lathe can make quick and very smooth work of this process. I can generally get them pretty close without that, and I have lots of sanding pads lying around to help the process.

I've built a few bikes without a front brake, but it always makes me feel uneasy - so much stopping power comes from the front brake, I wouldn't want to be out there with the "cagers" without one.

that has been dipped in lapping paste in a drill and create interesting fish-scaled designs on any flats you choose. Keep in mind though it is probably best to keep this idea for smaller parts, as doing a whole cam cover would take forever!

Because the Bird hardtail I chose does not create a straight line down the backbone of the frame, I had an interesting problem to deal with. The space between where the fender would be mounted, and the area where the front of the seat would be mounted were at two significantly different angles. There were a few ways to deal with this issue. I could have built a seat pan that was shaped to conform to the angle created by the slope in the frame. If I went this route, the best thing to do would have been to create a seat that had an increased amount of foam padding to fill the low spot in the frame. I didn't think that this was going to be a very comfortable proposition.

Initially I decided to leave the fender mounts on the front legs in case I wanted to run a front fender on a trip, or if I wanted to fab up a fork brace for another bit of detail work. I can always take off the forks and smooth these out the same way if I decide to later.

But then I do like a clean front end. I couldn't help myself, I broke out the band saw and removed the fender mounts. I'll live with the rain if I'm out riding.

Alternatively, I could have used seat springs on the cross member on the Bird hardtail to attach the rear of a seat. With this method, I would have had to use a mount that was welded to the center of the flat area at the upper connection between the hardtail and the original frame. I had originally settled on this idea, because I had planned from the start to use a Biltwell seat on this project. Upon initial mockup, I found that I would have to mount excessively tall springs on the seat to make up for the drop in the hardtail based on where I wanted the front mount. If I didn't use tall springs, the seat would have bottomed out on the top of the frame. This wasn't going to work either, as I didn't like the look of the super tall springs. In the end, I decided that I would fabricate a sort of sub-frame to attach the seat to the

The brake mount has to stay, but I will clean up everything else with a grinder and sanding disc. Its going to take a bunch of work to make it look like the fender mounts were never there.

frame. This would allow me to position the seat at the proper angle, along with mount the rear fender without using a sissy bar.

I try to use as small a fender as is humanly possible when I build a custom. I also try to make sure that they actually work as they are supposed to - that is, protect the rider from any flying debris. In the case of this build, I basically cut a fender blank to size that would end dead center at the top of the wheel. And because I wasn't planning on making this a fender that could support a human, I didn't have to worry too much about the strength of the mounts besides holding up the fender itself. If I do use a sissy bar, I try to make sure that the angle that it sits at matches that of some other angle of the frame. Because I didn't want to use a large fender, and because I wanted to center the mounting bungs on the fender itself, I couldn't find a matching angle on the frame that I liked for the angle of the sissy bar. Also, I had decided to use a fender blank from Led Sled that had a raised center section that would not allow for a clean fitting seat pan. Because of this, I decided that the solution was a component that combined the two parts.

To create the sub frame, I needed to build a skeleton that would provide for the proper angle for mounting the seat, as well as position the fender in such a way as to

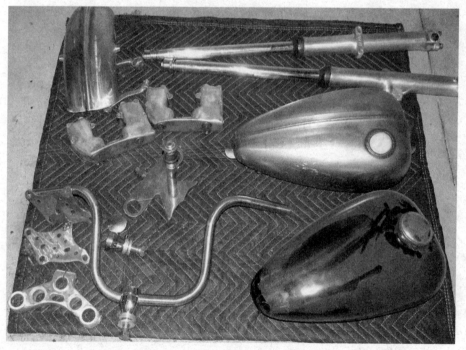

After a quick check of fitment of the motor in relation to the new subframe (something I should have done in the first place), the bike was disassembled and the frame prepped for powder coat.

float over the wheel in approximately the same place I'd planned to have it sit with the sissy bar. You can go about this in two different ways. First, you could place the seat and the fender in their locations and measure precisely as to where you will need to angle the sub frame in conjunction with the mounting points of both the frame and the fender. You would then need to cut and weld pieces together to create the finished product. I decided that this was more math than I wanted to try to tackle. Because the bends would be on different planes, creating two sides exactly the same would be a challenge without the construction of a jig. The second alternative was to use bar stock and my oxy-fuel torch and bend a sub frame one side at a time into the appropriate shape. This method would not produce two perfectly equal sides, but adjustments could be made that would be nearly imperceptible if the areas of applied heat during bending were approximately the same. Besides, because the two sides would be a fender-width apart, it would be even harder to tell if they were not exactly symmetrical. I decided to use the second method, even though it would take some time to "eyeball" fixes, and would require the reinstallation of both seat and fender multiple times to ensure proper fitment.

I began by bending a length of bar stock into an angle that was approximately the same as the triangle formed by the three mounting points at the bottom of the seat. I needed to take into consideration those three points as well as the two mounting holes for the hardtail that would be located directly under the seat. My plan was to create a mount that utilized those mounting holes to serve as the connection between the frame and the sub frame.

Once I had the initial "triangle" of the sub frame figured out, I had to fabricate both a mounting point for the connection to the frame, as well as the slight bend in the sub frame that would accommodate the angle of the rear seat mounts. After taking into consideration the connection between the frame and the hardtail, I decided that it would be best if I did not attach

I have a small sandblaster. At some point I'll probably invest in a cabinet-style sandblaster to minimize the mess. Generally, bigger items go to a shop, but I wanted to spot clean a few critical areas.

I also took some time to clean up some of the other parts I was going to take in for powdercoat. Always be sure to wear eye-protection when using air tools, and never wear flip-flops in your shop!

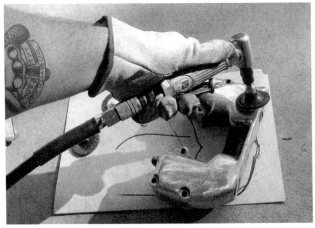

The die grinder and some surface conditioning discs do wonders on cleaning up old rusty rocker boxes.

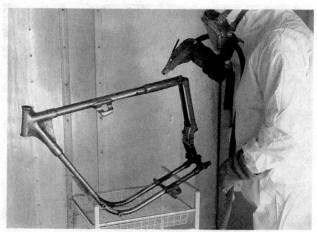

After repairing some welds and filling holes, I took a pile of parts over to Mike at Pro-Custom Powder Coating in Andover, MN. He sandblasted all of the parts for me in preparation for powder coat.

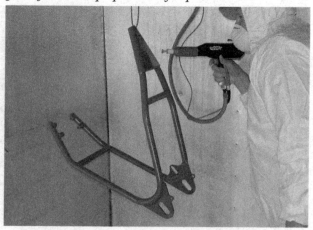

A thorough cleaning and a pre-heat in the oven, and it's time for Mike to apply the powder coat to the Ironhead parts. They received a primer coat first...

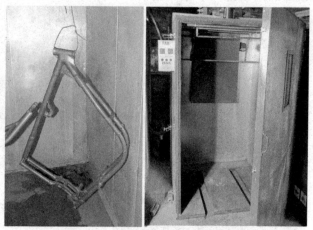

...and then a finish coat for a coating that is as smooth as liquid paint. Next, it's into the oven the parts will go. Smaller parts can be coated in your own home if you can come up with an oven.

the seat to both frame bolts. I chose this because I wanted at least one of the bolts to secure the frame and tail exclusively for safety. The secondary bolt would attach the seat to the sub frame as well as the sub frame to the frame itself.

Because I would be unable to attach a wrench to the bolt underneath the seat, I decided to weld a tab onto the bolt itself. This way, the heavy gauge metal slot that the bolt would slide in would provide a stop so the bolt would not move if the nut were removed from the underside of the frame. I welded a tab onto the bottom of the triangle that would connect both frame bolts to the sub frame. I then welded a tab onto the top of the sub frame that would serve as the connec-

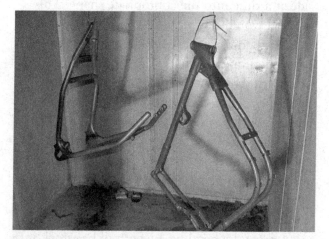

Here's the frame and tail in its finished color. Be sure your powdercoater fills in any mounting holes with tape so that you don't have to spend forever re-tapping the threads.

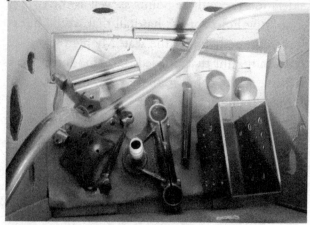

Along with the frame, I had various small parts sent in for powdercoating as well. Often if you take in a batch of work, you can get a reduced price on the whole project.

tion between the front seat bolt and the sub frame itself. As I was hard-mounting the seat, it did not matter that the seat was not going to pivot. After I had a solid mount for the sub frame, and the front of the seat was centered and mounted in the front, I again used my torch to heat up both sides of the sub frame to take into account the rear seat mounts. I bent both sides up and in towards the centerline of the frame to accomplish this. I was able to cut a couple of pieces of tubing that could be welded to the sub frame for the rear seat mounts. Once properly located by actually inserting the mounting bolts, I tack welded them in place for future final welds.

Because I try and match lines when fabricating, I wanted the sub frame to follow the lines of the tail section. After making sure the mounts I'd welded onto the sub frame for the rear of the seat were properly aligned, I once again took to the torch. I bent the sub frame down on each side to align with the frame, stopping at a point that would place the mounting bungs at the center of the fender (with the fender being placed atop some tubing to give it the proper location away from the rear wheel). I then cut off the sub frame to accept mounting bungs. I tacked the bungs on the fender and the sub frame in place and installed the seat and fender to ensure proper fit.

Once the seat and rear fender were properly mounted, it was time to mount the gas tank and oil tank. I chose a ribbed gas tank from Cycle Standard that matched the ribbed rear fender for this project. The easiest method for mounting this particular tank would be to drill two holes directly through the backbone of the frame. Unfortunately, this creates a weak spot in the frame that could cause cracking, and potentially frame failure. The better alternative is to drill out holes in the top of the frame that are large enough to allow threaded bungs to be welded in.

Unfortunately for me, the diameter of the bung was larger than the size of drill bit my drill would hold. If you have a stubby step-bit for a drill, you can get pretty close to the right size and then file out the remaining material for a tight fit.

After the frame comes back I check to make sure all the mounting points are clear of powdercoat. I like to run a tap through all the threaded holes. Next I can begin the process of reassembly.

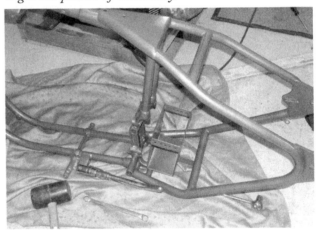

I've mounted all of the accessories that need to be accessed from the underside of the frame. Once the motor goes in, you wont want to have to reach under there to tighten anything up.

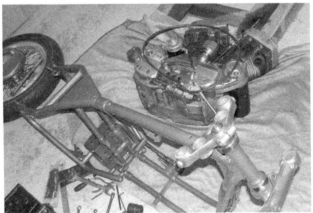

If you work alone, it is best to lay the motor on its side and place the frame over it. Then install the mounting bolts and turn it upright. Be sure to tape any of the areas that might be scratched in the process.

With motor, wheels and bars installed, I check to ensure I like how it's coming together. Plus I like to daydream about how fun the Ironhead is going to be to ride!

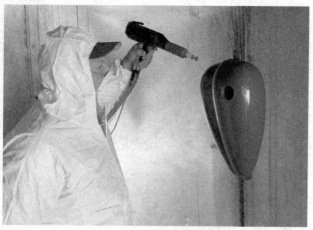

I decided to have the tank and fender powder coated as well as the frame. Here is the tank in the primer stage.

A close-up of the sharpest pinstripe tape angles on the tank

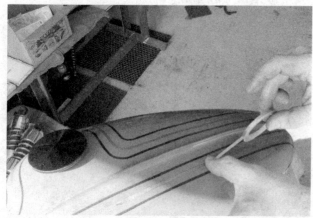

It's a pretty basic procedure to apply tape, you just need to get started at the right angle - and you can make some fairly straight lines. Be sure to wipe off your surfaces with alcohol before you start to provide a clean base for the tape.

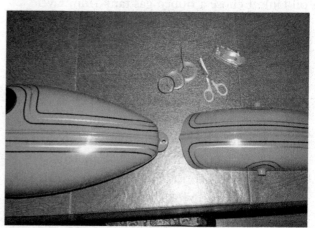

The finished product. You can get fairly sharp angles with the tape if you reshape the line progressively. Just watch and make sure you don't get ridges or bubbles in the line. It takes some care not to break the tape on sharp turns as well, but fixing a mistake is as easy as it gets.

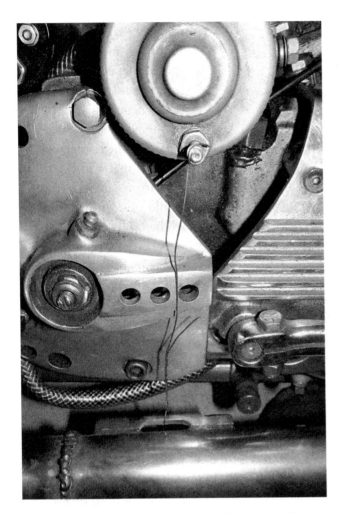

I wired the exhaust into place and began considering the best way to do a proper mount. I decided on utilizing the bottom sprocket cover bolt as a mounting point.

To figure out the right placement for the tank, it's always a good idea to install your front end to check for clearance. Of course this is assuming you already have fork stops installed. If not, you can adjust whatever method of fork stop you choose to clear the tank. Keep in mind that you may have very limited turning ability if you miscalculate here. I placed the tank far enough back to clear my forks, and drilled my mounting holes. Once I had the holes properly sized for a snug fit for the bungs, I tack welded them in place, double checked the fit, and finalized the welds.

Fitting the oil tank was more of a challenge to fit on this build than would normally be the case. The reason for this is that I chose to use an

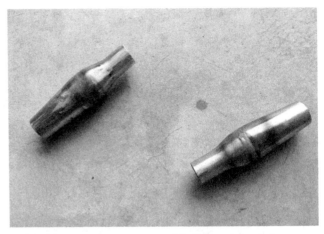

I felt like practicing, so I welded these up with my oxy-acetylene torch. They don't look pretty after all of the heat exposure, but once I hit them with a surface-prep disc, they will clean up nicely.

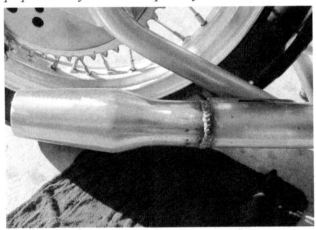

The new exhaust tip finished and welded to the pipe. As you can see, I basically cut the beginning and end off the muffler and welded them together. I have already smoothed the weld from the muffler down, but have not yet taken care of the weld to the pipe.

On the rear exhaust, I am going to use a clamp that bolts on to the rear triangle.

With the tank and fender finished, its time to get back to the assembly of the Ironhead. The motor in the frame, the tank mounted, the bars where they should be and the subframe awaiting oil tank and fender. At this point I've mounted the pipes I'm going to use for this build minus the chopped mufflers.

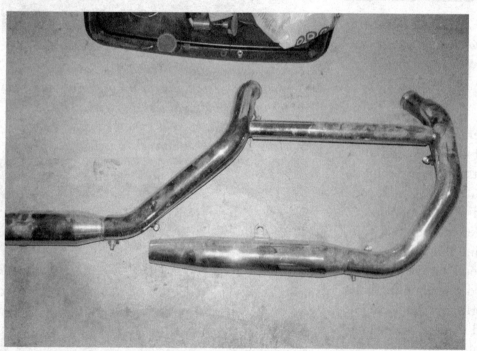

The chopped mufflers come from these. Sportsters wore these mufflers, they show up at swap meets all the time. All it takes is a hacksaw or band saw, a welder, and some sanding after the fact. You can choose how much of the center section you want to leave on the mufflers, but I generally cut them pretty short.

oil tank that had bungs pre-mounted on it that weren't specifically compatible to my frame. I had inadvertently begun this "ribbed" theme with both the gas tank and the fender, and I thought that a ribbed oil tank from 7 Metal West would be a fitting addition to the build. Actually, I won this tank in a raffle a few years back while I was still living in New Hampshire, and I just hadn't had found a particular build to use it on until now. The problem was that the two mounting bungs that were centered on the oil tank would conflict with the two tubes that ran down behind the engine. The oil tank bungs were spaced slightly wider than the center of each down tube, so it was not an option to just drill and mount. I could have welded bungs to the side of both down tubes, but that would have pushed the oil tank off center. So instead, I chose to add the oil tank mount onto the sub frame I'd built for the seat and rear fender.

Because the shape of the sub frame was already dictated by the seat and fender, I needed to create a downward facing, Y-shaped arm from which to mount the oil tank. I accomplished this by tacking together two pieces of the same bar stock I'd used for the sub frame, heating them with my torch, and bending them outward until they reached the

A few shots of the nearly finished product. I have a few things to button up on this one. A little wiring that will be hidden in the frame, oil line routing, cleaning up those cables a bit, and mounting some foot pegs and handgrips and she's good to go. The more I look at the exhaust, the more I think I should have . . .

proper width. I then heated the bottom portion of the piece and bent the bottom arm in a forward arc to provide for a surface to mount a piece of flat stock. This piece would fit directly between the two frame tubes so that the oil tank could be situated as close as possible to the two down tubes.

Because this was an organically formed part, it took a few reheats to make it fit correctly. Once I was confident that the fit was correct, I welded the y-section to the sub frame. I actually made this section with the engine out of the frame, and it caused me a bit of a headache later on in the build. My measurements for the actual space I had between the rear cylinder and the down tubes were incorrect, forcing me to reheat the y-section and bend it further back towards the rear. Once all three components attached to the sub frame were properly fit, it could be broken down and cleaned up. This piece could have been chromed or powder coated, but I felt that it would be a cool part to be left to get a patina of its own through time, so I cleaned up the welds and called it finished.

Since everything related to the frame and sheet metal was complete, I could begin to con-

. . . angled them up to match the rise of the rear triangle. If you see me on the road, it might look a little bit different next time. A project is never really done!

I cut my own spacers out of round stock I get from my metal supplier. If you have a means to cut them, its cheaper than buying wheel spacers kits.

sider finishes. Even though I have the ability and means to paint at my shop, I generally choose to send this work out due to time constraints and lack of the magical ability to do a good job. Because both motorcycles in this book were being completed at the same time, I decided it would be more cost-effective to send everything out to be finished together. I've found that you can usually get a pretty good discount by taking a large batch of parts to a shop for finish. This decision left me with a couple of options. I could either send everything out for paint, which would allow me a wider selection of color choices and design but be significantly more expensive. Or, I could save money and send everything to powder coat, which would create a more durable finish but lack much of an artistic impact.

Previous to these two builds, I'd never had tanks or fenders powder coated. In the case of frames, I'd had both painting and powder coating done depending on the project. Because one of my goals for this book is to show the reader some less expensive routes to produce a custom motorcycle, I chose to have all of my parts powder coated. Ultimately I knew that the powder coated bodywork could quite easily be pinstriped or have decals applied, so I feel like I made the right choice for these builds.

Of course you might be saying, "painting it myself" is the cheapest route. And with that I'd

My pushrod tubes were part of the lot that I sent to powder coat. It was cheaper to have them re-coated than it was to buy new ones.

agree - in some cases. You could head down to the local auto parts store and buy a few cans of primer and paint, as well as some supplies to fill and sand imperfections- and produce a fairly passable, if not great paint job. Bear in mind though that as with anything in the home-builder's world- a professional should have the experience to do the job you are undertaking more efficiently and in most cases with better tools at their disposal. If you are going to paint your own motorcycle, you need to be aware that preparation is more important than the painting itself. With both paint and powder coat, imperfections and impurities on the surface being fin-

Some leather washers help protect the fuel tank mounts from cracking.

The generator-mount regulator from Cycle Electric really helps to clean up the electrical system.

ished cause issues with adhesion- which can lead to an unstable finish. Along with that, the quality of finish materials is very important, with there being some brands whose quality control is not up to the standards of others. I learned this first-hand with the Ironhead project presented in this book. The frame was powder coated twice because the first powder, though the color I wanted, flaked right off the frame for no apparent reason. The powder coater and I had numerous conversations trying to figure out flaws in the technique that may have caused the issue, and could not. The only issue we could come up with was that the powder used was from a brand that he had never used before, and displayed inconsistencies with other reputable product. That is the sign of a professional to me. Somebody that tries to

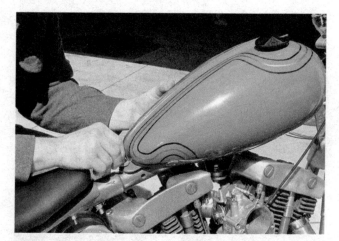

Mounting the fuel tank.

The underside of the seat showing the tail-section. You can see where the oil tank mount passes through the two downtubes.

The two mounting bolts for the hard tail. As soon as everything is mounted correctly, I will cut them to length, or find appropriate sized bolts without the excess length.

figure out the variable that caused the problem, in order to avoid making the mistake again.

Not to say that every "pro" out there is as experienced as the next in either the painting or powder coating worlds. More than once I've had friends take work to so-called professionals that came back with disappointing results. Unfortunately, I've found that a small number of the people who advertise themselves as professionals are really just amateurs trying to make a quick buck. Be wary of shops that seem to have lots of flash but not much substance. If they can't answer your questions, you should probably look elsewhere for somebody to handle your work.

No matter which route you choose, be sure to do your research and find somebody that is reputable and that you trust to do the work that you require. Both painting and powder coating are labor-intensive processes that require staying within certain parameters to create a quality finish.

Detail of the fender mount. I like the organic look of them, but may clean them up more at some point.

This particular XLCH had the magneto switched out to a points distributor. If I ever decide to go back to the magneto, it would be an easy switch.

Because I had the tank and fender powder coated, I wanted to add something that gave it a little more style than the single color provided. I could have taken the tank to be pinstriped by a professional, but I happened to have some 3M pin striping tape sitting around that I'd never used on anything. I figured I could try out a few designs, and if I didn't like it, no big deal. I could always peel it off without having harmed my tank finish, and have the tins pinstriped later on. I decided that I would follow the lines of the ribbing on the tank and fender and see what I could come up with for a design as I went. The tape itself is actually pretty easy to work with. You just need to make sure that you have a clean surface to begin with, and you can start laying down lines as you see fit. I started towards the back of the tank and worked my way around the edges,

Try to hide wiring as much as possible. In this case, I will solder extension wires onto the leads from the headlight and run them through the frame.

Twisting the wires before is a minor detail that makes unsightly wires look better.

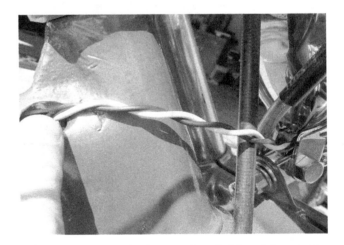

The wiring was a little too soft to hold a tight spiral. Some ideas just don't work the way you plan. I might just find some shrink tubing instead.

I went old-school on the fork stops. Rather than use stops welded to the triple tree, I decided to cut some lengths of chain to limit fork movement.

using the shape of the tank as my guide. The nice thing about working with the tape is that you can easily back up your line if you make a mistake. You just pull it up, and reposition it as you move along. I actually got a pretty good rhythm going of leading the tape roll around with one hand, and pressing the tape to the tank with the index finger of my other. Tight corners were a bit of a challenge, but setting and resetting the tape allowed me to pull it around without any ripples. It turned out to be a pretty simple and cheap detail to the motorcycle as a whole.

Once the tins were all powder coated and pinstriped, it was time to begin the reassembly process. With this build having been powder coated, you need to begin by giving some attention to any threaded surfaces that might need tapping to allow for proper fastening. I also used a razor or small rotary tool to take care of any build up of powder coat in places that needed to be bare metal. Once that was completed, I could go about putting the frame back together. I aligned the tail section with the frame, and mounted the battery box on the lower frame connection point. It is important that I reassembled the motorcycle in proper order, because some of the mounts would be nearly unreachable if I missed a step and jumped

The finished "fork stops". I'll do some strength testing of the chain to see if it can withstand the rigors of the road. If not, I can move up to a stronger chain.

Detail of the oil tank mount at the end of the downward arm on the subframe.

The ribbed oil tank I won at the Greasebag Jamboree in 2008 or so. Its about time I got around to using it on a build!

My kicker arm is going to rest on the exhaust pipe now that the stock oil tank is out of the way. As long as it doesn't rattle, I'm going to let it ride. I could always remove it since I have electric start, but I prefer taking the chance of dislocating my knee- it just looks cooler.

ahead. Because of my battery box being mounted on the same bolts that were attaching the hardtail to the frame, I was unable to use the safety washers that were supplied with the hardtail kit. Because of that, I made sure to use thread locker on all four of the bottom bolts. Once the bottom of the frame was secure, I could install the motor. This procedure is made most simple by laying the motor on its side, loosely attaching all of the motor mounts, and sitting it upright to finish securing the motor. Once completed, I was able to attach the front fork and both wheels so that I had my project sitting at its riding height.

Because the sub frame that I built was integral to the upper hardtail attach-

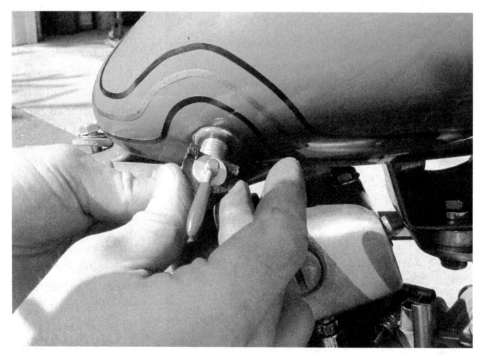

Installing the petcock on the fuel tank. My tank has petcock threads on each side of the tank, I can either run one and a plug, or use two and join the lines with a Y-connector.

Adjusting the lifters in preparation for the first post-rebuild run. Not too long now!

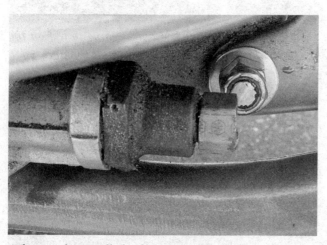

The poorly installed oil pressure switch plug, that I will replace with original working parts. It was a cheap fix that needed to be upgraded.

I removed the speedometer, and the previous owner ran a speedo off the front wheel. I decided to pick up a speedo plug to fix an unsightly issue.

ment point, it necessitated proper order of assembly. The oil tank mount actually weaved through the frame, so it had to be placed properly before any of the other accessories could be attached. Once the sub frame was in place, I could loosely attach the oil tank, and attach the front seat mount. I could then tighten down the sub frame in its correct location. The fender is the last part of this process, and it fit snugly between the mounting bungs, and was tightened down.

With the sub frame in place, and the motor mounted properly, I could address the exhaust fabrication. With this exhaust I wanted to use a trick I'd seen used somewhere of cutting the center section out of a stock muffler to create an exhaust tip. Basically all I did was take two stock mufflers, measure an equal distance up each, and cut them off. I then measured up the other end of both the mufflers and made sure the diameter was the same with my caliper before cutting off the other end. It doesn't have to be exact, and I noticed that the mufflers were slightly out of round, but it is a good idea to have the diameters of both cut sections be as close as possible for welding.

Once I had the two outer sections cut off, I removed all of the internal baffling to prepare them for welds. I took the sanding wheel to all edges that were to be welded to remove the chrome. I then checked to make sure that the pieces aligned properly before tack welding them together. Once I made sure that they were tacked together appropriately, I finished welding up the tips. For the rest of the exhaust, I used a couple of drag pipes that I cut to length to accept my newly created tips. Because my hardtail was bolted to the mounting point that previously held the stock exhaust bracket, I was forced to go a different route for mounting. I chose to mount both pipes to separate locations of the frame.

The front pipe would be secured by using the original mounting tab on the pipe and a small mount that would connect to one of the lower sprocket cover mounting holes. To accomplish this, I took a small ruler and measured the approximate distance between the mounting bracket on the pipe, and the sprocket cover bolt hole. Because the mount on the back of the pipe allowed for adjustment back and forth, I didn't have to be exact with the length of the mount I was creating. I cut two short pieces of tubing that were the same inside diameter as the bolts I was using. I then cut a short piece of bar stock that would be used to connect the two pieces of tubing. Next I welded the three pieces together, making sure that the two pieces of tubing aligned properly with one another. Because the exhaust pipe sat approximately a half-inch out from the sprocket cover bolt hole, I took the oxy-fuel torch and formed a slight S-shaped bend in the bar to accommodate the difference. Then I installed the mount, checked to make sure it fit properly and bolted it down. For the rear exhaust pipe, because I didn't weld a mount on to the frame before it was powder coated, I took a small 1.25" tubing clamp, and placed it in a position close to the rear pipe mounting point. I then fabricated another barbell shaped mount that was then secured to both the exhaust pipe and the tube clamp.

Once the exhaust was taken care of, I was able to complete the assembly of the rest of the project. I reinstalled the fuel tank using a couple of bolts and some leather washers that are great for giving a small amount of play to the tank to prevent any cracking of welds at the tank mounts. To prevent the fork from hitting the tank on turns, I decided to attach a couple of chains to each side of the fork that would run to a section of threaded rod that I ran through a mounting hole on the frame.

Basically I just cut some chain to length based on the maximum fork travel I wanted to allow, and ran a bolt through one end into a threaded hole that was original to the fork. I then cut the threaded rod to length and tightened a bolt down on each side of the frame. I inserted the chain, and then added a secondary bolt to finish up the old-school fork stop. This is the first time I've used the method, even though I've seen it on a lot of choppers. If I don't like it, or find

Bolting the Biltwell seat onto the subframe.

The Biltwell seat installed on the subframe. It looks like it was made to be there.

Reinstalling the PM front brake. When I first put it back together I was having clearance issues. I went back and realized I had placed some spacers incorrectly.

The rear fender installs fairly easily between the sub-frame arms.

A close-up of the Biltwell risers. Classy looking parts right there!

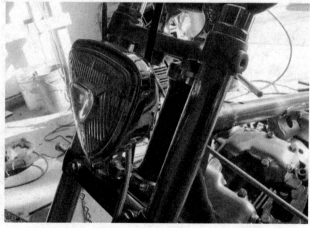

The Aris-style headlight mounted on the triple tree.

that the chain is rubbing on the frame during travel, I can always alter the triple tree to accept fork stops later on without visibly altering any powder coated parts.

The bars I used were actually on the original motorcycle when I purchased it. I'm not 100% where they came from, but to me they look to be older Front St. Cycle bends. Either way, I really liked them from the start, so I had them powder coated, along with the frame, to be reused. I mounted them to some Biltwell risers, and finished of the front end with a reproduction Aris headlight I picked up. I cleaned up an old front master cylinder and lever I had, as well as a mechanical clutch lever and mounted them to the handlebars.

With the exception of running a few oil and fuel lines, all that remained unfinished on the Ironhead was wiring. I am not going to spend a whole lot of time talking about that, because there thankfully isn't a whole lot to do! I will mention that whenever I work with Ironheads, I almost always remove the old square regulator in favor of the generator-mounted style. It gives a much cleaner look to the motorcycle, and reduces a couple of unsightly wires. Beyond that, it comes down to running a few wires for the headlight, taillight, the distributor and the starter. I usually hide the junctions somewhere inconspicuous (In the case of the Ironhead it will be either in the headlight, or under the battery), so as to show as little wiring as possible.

After that, it comes down to checking the timing and adjusting the pushrods, adding some fluids and I should be good to go!

The finished project (minus one pushrod tube if you have a good eye - yes I dropped it and chipped it last minute. We all make mistakes!) … Otherwise this project is ready to hit the road!

Chapter Seven

Ironhead Performance

Cast Iron Horses

When you are building an Ironhead project, you have three areas to consider: power, handling, and cosmetics. When it comes to performance, the cosmetic aspect of the build can't be overlooked. Cosmetically, you can shave weight by using lighter materials and removing unnecessary components. This will have some level of effect on the performance of your motorcycle. However, when it comes to really dramatic changes in performance, you need to address the power your motor is providing, and how that power is transferred to the road. In the case of an Ironhead, this gets a little tricky. As with any alteration that takes your motorcycle away from stock, there are going

The DP Café Racer with all of its old-school cool. I really like the squared off look.

to be people on both sides of the argument as to whether you should proceed. But with an Ironhead, in many cases you are dealing with something that is now considered an antique - which makes for an even wider grey area. The following will provide you with some information you can use to choose how you want to increase the performance of your Ironhead.

ENGINE MODIFICATIONS

Engine modifications are one of the areas where I would suggest you leave much of the work up to the professionals. I say this only while considering that the tools you need to do a quality job are usually outside of the financial reach of the garage builder. It could be said however that engine modifications should be the place to start if you want a high performance Ironhead. I would certainly consider head work as the first step in the engine hop-up process. Think of it this way; if the internal mechanisms of your motor are not running and flowing efficiently, why would you think that anything external would provide much help in building power? Porting can increase power drastically in an engine. By using a flow bench, a porter can measure the flow of air through your cylinder heads. Their goal is to find the optimal amount of flow through the heads. In order to get to this optimal level of flow, the person doing the porting removes imperfections by grinding, sanding and polishing away inconsistencies. They continually smooth and test, until that optimal level of flow

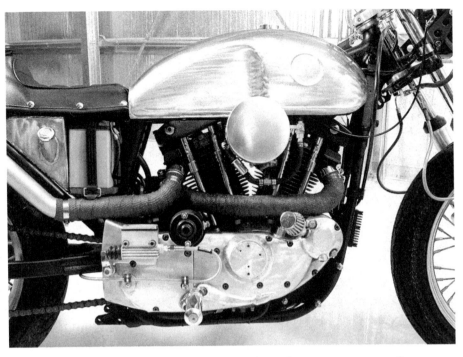

The engine area of another DP Customs café racer. Nice knee indentations on the tank.

Side view of the DP Customs café racer. Very clean interpretation of the style.

A Performance Machine break set up on the rear of Jeff Wright's Sportster. A nice upgrade from stock. Oh, and notice the safety wire!

is reached. When you consider that no matter what modifications you do otherwise to increase the flow of the fuel-and-air mixture through your engine, your heads are responsible for "processing" that mixture. If they are not efficient and free-flowing, the other modifications you perform will never live up to their abilities.

A bit of warning to anybody who might consider having this process done. First, there are a lot of shops that advertise that they port and polish heads. Making sure you find a reputable shop is key. Consider this, a tuner shouldn't polish everything to a fine finish - it actually has negative effects on flow. If your tuner does this, he probably isn't as experienced as another shop would be. Even though I don't know where you as the reader live in relation to some of the better tuning shops in the country, I would suggest you not be afraid to mail your heads out to a tuner rather than stay local. Heads are fairly small and can be boxed and shipped out readily. Also, heads can be picked up on EBay for a fair price, so you could actually buy a second set and have those ported while you continue riding your Ironhead as is. Do a little checking online, and see who comes up as a reputable shop. If you choose to send them across the country, so be it. Then again, you might get lucky and find someone near you that gets great reviews, and will do a great job.

Beyond head work, you can get into some engine modifications that will also build power, but might not have as much of an effect if you don't actually port and polish your heads. Most obvious would be changing you cams into something a little "hotter". Some cams will actually do quite a bit without head work, but a combination of both is always going to make more power if done correctly - the person doing

A custom exhaust built for the DP Customs Ironhead. Looks like something off of a modern day race bike.

110

There's nothing wrong with running the good old CV carb.

questionable, I often recommend against boring out cylinders unless necessary for a repair. I personally believe there are better ways to build power than inching up on the edge of safety by boring out a motorcycle being used on the street. Some very specific issues arise when you start sizing up your pistons. Among other things, Ironhead cylinders have oil return lines within the cylinder walls. If you bore the cylinder out too far, you run the risk of exposing the oil line area. Some might say that boring cylinders is relatively cheap compared to other options, though I tend to disagree. If you are going this route, there's no

the headwork may recommend a certain set of cams.

Cams generally effect one area of power over another, so if you want low end grunt you choose one cam, if you want a higher-revving motor, you choose another. Also note that there are cams that have duration that is not suited to street use. Don't be afraid to consult one of the many websites out there for additional information. Do your research as to which cam will do what you prefer given your specific motor. Cams are fairly easily installed yourself if you have a service manual and some time. Also, with some cams you will need to address the installation of new valve springs that will control valve travel. Again, however, if you are doing some combination of engine work on your Ironhead - you might want to seek a professional.

Because some Ironhead parts are becoming scarce, and because I think the cost-effectiveness is

The Performance Machine four piston caliper I used on the front of the Ironhead build. It stops well, and is easy to set up.

sense in not doing other additional work - porting and polishing, and a cam change.

A stroker kit falls into the same category as boring in terms of price and performance, but again you are entering an area of diminishing returns when you invest in these high-dollar services on a street-use motorcycle (assuming you didn't do all the other work mentioned previously). Plus, Ironheads with excessively long stroke don't tend to do too well in real world street situations. A lot of people are probably going to disagree with me on this one, but of the motor modifications I mentioned, boring and stroking for

street use tend to create more problems than they fix if you haven't already invested in other hop ups. So as I see it, head work provides proven flow improvements that can provide horsepower in and of itself (especially when the carb and exhaust are tuned to match). Cams will provide a different powerband that can react well with stock or modified intake and exhaust. Boring and stroking should be left to the Ironhead race motors, or be prepared to deal with other issues if you go that route.

Another thing to consider before you get started in the motor modification process is price. I firmly believe that if you are really concerned about building more power from you engine, you should know that porting and polishing is going to cost in the neighborhood of $500-$1000 depending on the shop. When you consider that this has the potential to add around 20% more

An old-school springer fork I have had for some time. It doesn't exactly hold the road like some of the new springers do.

About the shortest drag pipe baffle you can buy. In a state I used to reside in, unbaffled drag pipes were illegal. Everybody would put these in to give the illusion that they were actually running baffled pipes. They did nothing to quiet the roar.

power if done correctly, it stands to be one of the more reasonable modifications you can make. On the other hand, cams can be had for half that or less depending on where you find them. Labor can be next to nothing if you install them yourself. They will also provide significant power by themselves, and more so if combined with other modifications. Boring or stroking can be very expensive, and both methods perform better if you modify other aspects of your engine. Again, this is all opinion, but it should give you a better basis for a decision on motor modification.

INTAKE MODIFICATIONS

Intake modifications are a bit more cut and dry when it comes to the Ironhead motor. The intake manifold itself on an Ironhead is a simple pathway, though it can be cleaned up a bit much like the heads. In the case of carburetion, there are a few choices out there based upon personal preference. In some opinions, the two projects shown in this book probably could have their carburetors flip-flopped. The Ironhead project is running an S&S "E", while the Evo is running a Keihin CV (Constant Velocity). In fact, I feel that both are solid carburetors, and both can be effective on either motorcycle. I like how easy the S&S carb is to tune, and it provides solid performance on just about any application. That said, I wouldn't rule out other options including Bendix, Mikuni and SU. Bendix carbs can be a reliable stock option on an Ironhead. I generally don't use them on my builds, as they don't give the performance upgrade that an S&S or CV carb provides. I've found that the SU carbs can work really well, and can be found at swap meets or online for cheap. The downside to

The Ironhead project's S&S "E" carburetor. An easy to tune, better performing replacement for the stock carb.

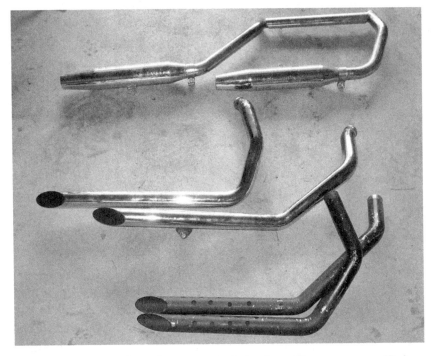

Some of the pipes I have laying around the shop. The top are muffled stock pipes, the middle are double walled drag pipes, the bottom are the worst idea the previous owner ever had!

them is that they do stick out quite a distance from the motor itself based on their design. The Mikuni is an option that I don't have a whole lot of experience with. I have used them the least of all the options I have listed here. I have seen both Mikuni and SU carbs used in dual-carb applications- which looks pretty awesome, and from all the information I've received, they can be as effective as the other models listed above in single or dual applications.

I generally use either S&S or some other aftermarket air cleaner in conjunction with my carb. I love the look of velocity stacks, as it allows the most access to viewing the motor, but I don't recommend them for daily riding. I'm sure plenty of people will disagree with me on this one, but even with a screen it seems to me that some pretty large particles can be sucked into the intake of an Ironhead. Consider as well that at speed, there is a

Even though they're on an Evo, remote reservoir rear shocks are available for Ironheads. They make a world of difference in bringing the rear end under control.

lot of turbulence around the intake that will not be reeled in with a velocity stack as it would with a shielded air cleaner. This can create a lot of "confusion" for a carb, and can make the engine run roughly. Lastly, it might be okay to bar hop on a motorcycle with stacks, but consider that during a long ride you run the risk of encountering rain: which will bring your motorcycle to a halt in a hurry. Save the velocity stacks for the shows, or bike night at the local bar.

All things considered, you have many options for effective intake on an Ironhead. If you do choose to do engine work in conjunction with intake changes, it is probably a good idea to seek out the advice of your performance shop to see which model they recommend. If you choose to go it on your own, keep your eyes open for the model you like at swap meets or online, and consult the manufacturer or the online forums for recommendations on jetting and setup.

EXHAUST MODIFICATIONS

Exhaust modifications on Ironheads in relation to performance are to me the most "magical" aspect of hop-up. Years ago, I read something that said that exhaust pipes that were 30" long were the magic number for performance on an Ironhead. I can't necessarily say whether that is true or false. I've used lots of aftermarket exhausts, and built just as many more that all performed well. I will say there are some guidelines that should be followed or at least considered when choosing an exhaust.

First of all, I hate drag pipes. They're loud, and they lose lots of power in street situations. All of their power comes in the high end of the power band. If you are building a track Sportster, absolutely use them. But if you plan to ride your Sporty on the street, do me a favor and ditch the drags in favor of something that will help put the big twin guys to shame! You need backpressure to build low-end power in a street-worthy Ironhead, so if you actually decide to run drags - you will need to baffle the pipes. It doesn't take a lot to solve some of the backpressure issue. I usually use 1 inch baffles, torque cones, or the old lollipop technique: which is drilling a hole towards the end of the exhaust to accept an eyebolt or thumbscrew

Dual-sided exhaust on a DP Customs Ironhead. It doesn't follow the grey-beard rule of having the pipes be the same length, but it sure looks cool. And my guess is that it performs just fine.

All in all, it seems to me that you could save some money and potentially increase your performance by building your own system.

If you are going to build your own exhaust system, you will need to keep a few things in mind. First of all, keep your bends smooth and fluid. Sharp bends produce hot spots that are detrimental to power and to the exhaust itself. Consider putting a muffler on the end of your pipes. If you are going old-school, consider the old trumpet or reverse trumpet mufflers. They aren't going to be as good as a full aftermarket exhaust, but at least you have some baffling and they will look period correct. One trick I've been using lately is to build a muffler section that fits around a standard drag pipe like a sleeve. I then attach mounts on both sections and attach the two by way of a spring(s), much like you see on a motocross bike. It also has a cool look, and is removable if you want to switch it up to another style. If you are going to run without a muffler, or want to leave the pipes short, consider trying torque cones. Torque cones function on the same principle as baffles, but are inserted between the exhaust port and the exhaust pipe, rather than

and nut. That usually provides enough turbulence to prevent reversion. Reversion being the action of exhaust gasses creeping back up the exhaust and into the intake valves due to changes in barometric pressure inside the cylinders. That concept all sounds pretty technical, but to those of us that have experienced it, it translates into a flat spot in low-end acceleration.

If you are going to buy an exhaust, you have somewhat limited "performance" options. Quite a few custom shops build Ironhead-specific exhausts, but most of them have not been tuned in such a way as to provide significant gains over something a home builder could do. The big-box retailers have Ironhead exhaust systems available, but most of them are essentially drag pipes, or drag pipes with a muffler extension. I have not had the opportunity to try it, but sportyspecialties.com advertises a 2-into-1 Ironhead exhaust that looks like it might have the potential to be a good option. Some people revert back to the Ironhead header pipes with crossover that came standard on some models and add aftermarket mufflers.

A close-up of the motor on the same motorcycle. Note the big easy breathing air cleaner and the exhaust splitting to both sides.

at the external end of the pipe. This allows you some freedom in terms of customization at the outlet end of the pipe.

HANDLING AND BRAKING

Most everything I've talked about in this chapter up to this point has been related to straight-line performance. But if you truly want a street-worthy performance Ironhead, it will need to handle as well as it runs. This is best accomplished with a balance of proper suspension, and strong brakes.

Most of the Ironheads that I have built have been hardtails. This has detrimental effects on the performance of the motorcycle in the sense that a motorcycle with a well tuned full suspension will handle far better than one that is only suspended at the front. Think of it this way, all that power

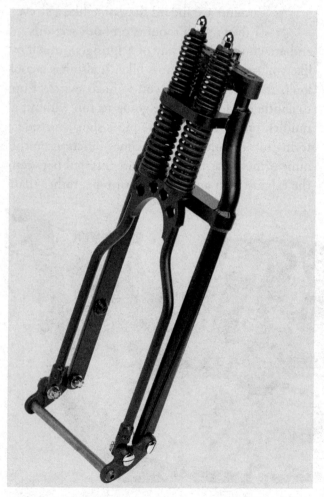

Led Sled Customs' springer is a modern-day interpretation of springers of old. Looks cool and performs well I'm sure.

you made by building up your engine needs to get to the ground to move you forward. If your rear tire is hopping up and down from torque, you are losing precious power transfer. I choose to give up some of that power for the sake of aesthetics and cool factor with a hardtail frame. But then again, I'm not going out there to try and set any land speed records. If I wanted to build a truly all-around street performance machine, I would certainly keep a swingarm frame and set it up with fully-adjustable rear shocks.

In front, you have a much wider range of options at your disposal. With machining skills, your choice of fork is nearly limitless. I've seen many people use late-model sport bike forks on old-school Ironheads. There are a couple of modern sport bike forks that only need minor machining to fit within an Ironhead neck. If you don't have access to a machine shop, or don't want an aggressive looking sport bike fork, you can use stock forks from many HD models with the proper adapters. In the aftermarket world, there's springer forks, leaf-sprung forks, hydraulic forks-whatever style you prefer, you can find one for an Ironhead. With the advances in engineering on all of these types of front suspension, most any of them can be made to perform effectively. The days of the bouncy, out-of-control springer are gone. That said, if you are trying to stay period-correct, or are building an out-there chopper, or are lucky enough to find a vintage springer or leaf-sprung fork, don't be afraid to use it. I've built a couple of motorcycles around forks I've found at swap meets, and as long as you understand the limitations, and ride accordingly, there's no reason you shouldn't use them.

When it comes to braking, you should always keep in mind that the bulk of your stopping power comes from the front brake. I'm pretty sure my old motorcycle permit handbook used to say 70-75% if I remember correctly. And in many cases, I'd imagine the number is probably much higher than that. If you don't have a front brake, you lose much of your ability to stop in a timely manner. Obviously, if you are going to use certain types of front end, your braking options are going to be more limited. If you use a springer fork, you have limited options when it comes to mounting a brake. There are lots of adapter kits out there, but most of them have a specific brake piston setup that they are engineered around. I have an old Hallcraft mini-drum brake setup in my shop that I had on an Ironhead chopper with a drum rear brake. Suffice it to say that was not a fun bike to ride in city traffic. I think I had about as much chance of slowing down that motorcycle with a gloved hand gripping the front tire as I did of stopping quickly with that little brake. The minimum I should have done on that particular motorcycle would have been to swap out the rear brake with a disc so that I had some chance to at least skid to a stop! Luckily there are some options out there these days to use modern brake calipers on springer forks. Check out fabkevin.com for some good examples of brake kits for use on springers.

On hydraulic forks, you can either use the brakes that came with that fork from the factory, or search the aftermarket for something with a little more stopping power. On the Ironhead in this book, I used a Performance Machine 4-piston front disc brake for its reliability and strong performance. Because the rear drum on the Ironhead isn't known to have the best stopping-power, I wanted to make sure that the front brake was going to do what it was designed for. Of course the choice of brakes is up to you, as there are lots of different options available out there - and if you are mechanically inclined, you can make an adapter for just about any caliper you can find.

One thing to remember when choosing a caliper for your front end is that in the case of hydraulic braking systems, you have to consider the hydraulic ratio between the master cylinder and the caliper(s).

Essentially you need to match the size of the master cylinder bore to the caliper(s). A smaller diameter master cylinder piston creates more hydraulic pressure, but displaces less fluid, than a larger diameter piston (all other things being equal). A bike with two, four-piston calipers on the front will likely need a master cylinder with a larger diameter piston (which will displace more fluid) than a similar bike with a single caliper. So

don't just bolt that master cylinder you bought cheap at the swap meet onto the handle bars - without first considering the diameter of the piston inside that master. Lots of advice can be found on line as to the best combinations.

After addressing suspension and stopping, I'm a firm believer in putting my Ironheads on a diet program to further enhance performance. Depending on the style of motorcycle you are going for, this may or may not be of importance to you. As I mentioned in an earlier chapter, I try to remove all things that are not critical to a build. I minimize electronic components, which on an Ironhead is relatively easy compared to late-model Sportsters. I remove as much material as possible as well, and opt for using the lightest sheet metal for fabrication that I can possibly get away with. I drill lots of "speed holes" to reduce material wherever it isn't necessary for strength. I like to think that there is some sort of race influence in all of my builds, whether or not the style calls for it!

Mikuni carburetor set up. I haven't used many of these, but those that have swear they're a great choice.

Chapter Eight

Tools

Tools of the Garage Builders Trade

Aside from the vast information available on the Internet, I did say I was going to mention some of the tools I use when working on a build. I will leave the basic hand tools out of this conversation minus the mention that you generally get what you pay for when it comes to these. I'm not saying you should spend top dollar to get the premium name brands. But I would make sure that wherever you buy your hand tools from, you get a lifetime warranty. These days even lower-priced tool companies have that warranty in many cases, so I leave preferences up to you.

Perhaps not a necessity, but when it comes to tools it's hard to overemphasize the importance of a good welder. Though a good TIG welder might seem outside your budget, smaller units designed for enthusiast and small-commecial shop have come onto the market in the last few years with price tags that start at a little more than $1000.00. Be sure to buy a brand name unit so you can get help and/or parts after the purchase.

The oxy-acetylene torch will be a friend to you. Buy whatever sized tanks you can afford. Since my shop is very near a welding supply store, I keep them small and transportable.

My shop doesn't look like much from the outside. But I can create just about anything I need with the tools I have inside.

Having multiple grinders makes your life much easier in the long run. You can get by with one, but you'll spend half your time changing wheels from project to project.

You'll eventually have quite the collection of wheels and discs for your electric and pneumatic grinders. Try and keep them more organized than this!

To start, without a doubt the tool I use the most in my shop is my assortment of grinders. I try to keep at least three of them at the ready at any given time. I generally have them set up in the same area of my shop, with a 3 into 1 outlet connecting them together. The first grinder will generally have a cutting wheel attached to it. Obviously, I use this for cutting metal parts, but I will often also use it to score metal for bending purposes. A shallow channel cut into metal and a couple of clamps on your workbench provide a simple and effective bending brake for the aspiring builder who doesn't have the funds or space to buy the real deal.

The second grinder in my arsenal will most often have a grinding wheel attached to it. This allows you to take a fairly aggressive approach to metal removal. This is the tool I use to blend and

One tank is compressed Oxygen...

The other is dissolved Acetylene. Together they can make things very hot in your shop.

The torch can be used to create fairly complex shapes through a method of heating and twisting. Try it on some hex bar if you get a chance. It can make for some really cool projects.

shape larger areas of metal that I've modified. From the removal of stock frame mounts, to taking down areas of the frame for the fitment of a hardtail, the grinding wheel is the go-to when it comes to removing metal in a hurry. Take care though; I generally like to make sure to stay around 1/8th of an inch away from finished levels when working with an aggressive grinder.

Last but not least is my finish grinder. This tool will generally either have a flap-style sanding disk, or a wire wheel attached to it. I use this for final blending or scale removal depending on which of the types of wheel I am using at the time. This is also the tool I use to prepare two surfaces for welding, as well as to blend welds after the fact. This is the grinder that you are going to use a bunch if you are using GMAW (Mig) as your method of welding.

When you are starting out, you can certainly get by with a single grinder. But you will find that through time, it is much easier to have a few set up versus spending time switching an endless number of disks. The grinders themselves aren't overly expensive generally priced anywhere from $50 to $100, and picking one up on sale can happen fairly frequently. As with hand tools, grinding wheels are a place where it is probably best not to pinch pennies. I have had the unfortunate experience more than once of having a knock-off grinding wheel explode off my grinder while working on a project. That's not to say it won't ever happen when using the more trusted industrial manufacturers (3M, Norton, etc.), but in my experience, the integrity of these wheels is usually much higher. And the price difference between quality industrial wheels is generally just a few dollars more than anything you'll find at the discount supply stores.

The tool that gets used nearly as often as my grinder is the oxy-acetylene torch. When it comes to an all-around useful garage apparatus, I can't think of something that I've purchased that has as many applications as my torch. I believe without a doubt that the oxy-acetylene torch should be the garage builder's first major shop purchase. With a couple of different tips, the torch allows you to

Some bends done with the torch on standard square tubing.

I use my GMAW welder on a daily basis. I can tack and weld just about anything related to a motorcycle project with this.

The flux-cored wire does better on the thick stuff, or when you aren't able to use a tank of shielding gas.

The inside door of most GMAW welders have a useful guide that gives you the proper setup parameters based on the thickness of the material you wish to weld.

Welding Guide for 115 Volt Wire Welding Package

Settings are approximate. Adjust as required. Thicker materials can be welded using proper technique, joint preparation and multiple passes.

Recommended Voltage and Wire Speed Settings for thickness of metal being welded. Number on left of slash is Voltage Setting / Number on right of slash is Wire Feed Setting

Material Being Welded	Wire Type and Polarity Setting	Suggested Shielding Gas 20-30 cfh Flow Rate	Diameter of Wire Being Used	24 ga. .024 in. (0.6 mm)	20 ga. .036 in. (0.8 mm)	18 ga. .048 in. (1.2 mm)	16 ga. .060 in. (1.6 mm)	11 ga. 1/8 inch (3.2 mm)	3/16 inch (4.8 mm)	1/4 inch (6.4 mm)	CHANGING POLARITY
Steel	Flux Cored E71T-11 (DCEN)	No Shielding Gas Required Good for Windy or Outdoor Applications	.030" (0.8 mm)	---	---	1/30	2/30	3/	4/45	---	**DCEN** Electrode Negative For Flux Cored Wire
			.035" (0.9 mm)	---	---	---	2/20	3/20	4/35	4/50*	
Steel	Solid Wire ER70S-6 (DCEP)	C₂₅ Gas Mixture 75% Argon / 25% CO₂ Produces less Spatter Better Bead Appearance	.024" (0.6 mm)	1/25	2/30	3/40	3/50	4/70	---	---	
			.030" (0.8 mm)	---	2/20	2/30	3/35	4/40	---	---	
			.035" (0.9 mm)	---	---	3/25	3/30	4/40	---	---	
Steel	Solid Wire ER70S-6 (DCEP)	100% CO₂	.024" (0.6 mm)	---	2/30	3/30	3/40	4/40	---	---	
			.030" (0.8 mm)	---	---	3/20	4/30	4/35	---	---	**DCEP** Electrode Positive For Solid Wire
			.035" (0.9 mm)	---	---	---	4/25	4/30	---	---	
Stainless Steel	Stainless Steel (DCEP)	Tri-Mix 90% He/7.5% Ar/2.5% CO₂	.024" (0.6 mm)	---	---	2/30	3/40	4/50	---	---	
			.030" (0.8 mm)	---	---	2/15	3/10	4/30	---	---	
Aluminum	Aluminum** (DCEP)	100% Argon**	.030" (0.8 mm)	---	---	---	3/90**	4/90**	---	---	

Match feedroll groove to diameter of wire being used. Set Tension Knob Setting to 3 at start. Adjust tension per instructions in the manual.

CAUTION! Do not change Voltage switch position while welding. See owners manual for more information.

Wire Speed listed is a starting value only. Wire Speed setting can be fine-tuned while welding. Wire Speed also depends on other variables such as stick out, travel speed, weld angle, cleanliness of metal, etc.

*Multiple passes required. **Aluminum wire is soft so feedability is not as good. Make sure that hub tension is not too tight and keep the torch straight as possible. A "push angle" for the torch is recommended.

217618-B

Most of the time I have solid wire in my GMAW gun, as I work indoors with thinner metal projects. It's a good idea to buy the smaller rolls if you don't weld on a regular basis, as the rolls can corrode over time and negatively effect your welds.

The 75% Argon, 25% Carbon Dioxide mix is the staple on my GMAW welder. It produces good results, but check with your local welding shop if you have questions on which gas to use.

bend, weld, braze and cut metal. On most of my builds, I like to incorporate some detail object that involves metal bent or twisted with the use of the gas torch. In both of the projects presented in this book, I used the gas torch to manipulate bar stock into shapes relevant to each build. As far as price goes for a torch setup, that can vary pretty drastically. I would suggest looking on websites for a used industrial-quality torch. You can often find entire rigs with tanks and all for a couple hundred dollars. Be aware though that certain restrictions apply to filling the tanks. And if they have not been pressure tested in some time, it may be more cost effective just to purchase or lease tanks at a welding supply.

Though not the most time-efficient method, the beginning builder should learn to weld with the gas torch. It isn't fast, and it can be a challenge to become proficient, but aspects of it are useful to know before tackling other forms of welding. Most specifically, the concept of moving the pool and adding filler with the other hand that can be learned with a gas torch are easily applied to the movements required when learning Gas Tungsten Arc Welding (GTAW) often known as Tig welding. I use this method from time to time mainly to stay in practice or when I am welding outdoors, but at this point I generally stick to other techniques to produce viable welds.

Brazing is a method of joining metal that may seem fairly outdated by some, but it has a very useful place in the garage builders skill set. With the purchase of the torch, it is another accessible method of joining material. Essentially, brazing is the method of heating a secondary filler material that has a lower melting point than the materials being joined. Where welding actually fuses two work pieces together by melting the base metal with a filler metal, brazing uses capillary action to fill "pores" that open when the base metal is heated, and adheres to those pores when the metal cools. Both welding and brazing produce strong bonds, In fact, on a production level, many vehicle frames are brazed rather than welded because it has minimal effects on the strength of the two pieces being joined. Welding in turn, if done improperly can create brittle areas or cracking where brazing would have had no ill effects. The flip side of that coin however, is that in brazing

Upgrading to a larger capacity compressor can be one of the best investments you make.

After just a few trips to the metal supply, you can start to gather a respectable amount of raw materials for projects.

only the filler material is melted - at somewhere above 840 degrees or so - which means it might not be suitable for high heat situations. In reality however, both methods can be effective if properly applied. From an artistic perspective, brazing can create some very interesting looking joints. Because of the capillary action, if the person brazing is properly skilled, very smooth joints can be produced, requiring little or no finishing.

Though I don't use the gas torch for welding very often, it did come in handy when filling a few of the holes left on the original Ironhead frame from previous customization. It can be used with practice and the right tips on just about any

My shop. Not exactly the most organized place, but I know where things are when I need them.

Some of the air tools you will find useful for your builds. Air saws, drills, die grinders, and wrenches all have a place in the home builder's toolbox.

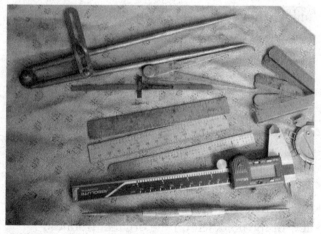

Measure twice, cut once. When working with metal, it can be a pricey mistake when you measure incorrectly.

thickness of metal. But if you have any of the electric-arc welders, you will generally find the ease of use and speed of those make them your go-to welder.

I don't do much actual cutting with my torch, though it is one of the many uses of the device. I mainly use mechanical means when I am cutting metal related to motorcycle projects. When it comes to thick plate, it can come in very handy, but your average vehicle doesn't have a lot of that to deal with. Also, because of oxidation issues an oxy-acetylene torch won't readily cut through aluminum or stainless. Regardless, the option is there for ferrous (iron-containing) metals if you happen to need it.

Third on my list of shop tools necessary for the burgeoning garage builder is the Gas Metal Arc Welder (GMAW) or "Mig" welder. To me, this is the obvious purchase choice for electric arc welding for many reasons. First of all, it is a relatively inexpensive machine to purchase. You can usually find a welder of this variety for less than $500 that will handle most all projects related to building a motorcycle. Second, it is the quickest method to becoming a relatively proficient welder. Once you understand the idea of the "pool" of molten material you are manipulating with the welder, using the GMAW welder becomes a process of setting the machine for your material, pulling a trigger and moving at the proper pace along your weld. Of course I'm oversimplifying the process, but with some practice you can become proficient at GMAW fairly quickly. Even though I have a GTAW machine in my welding arsenal, I find that I spend most of my time using the GMAW to this day. I like how quickly I can tack things up with Mig, as well as how quick it is to change between various types of welding wire for certain circumstances. I can easily switch between using flux-cored wire for thicker steel, to solid wire with a tank of gas for thinner material. In the case of the projects included in this book, I used a 115v welder to show that most any homebuilder can complete a Sportster project with a standard household-power welder. Along with that, I generally recommend that unless you really

You might not be able to afford a mill or a lathe when you first start out, but a good drill press is a great poor-man's way of doing things in a pinch.

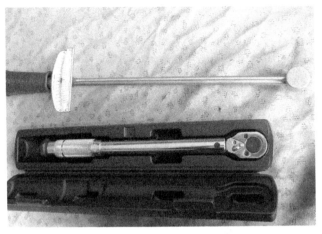

When you start getting into actual engine repair and customization, torque wrenches are important to have. Your service manual will have charts showing you torque specs for your model.

I may not have mentioned it much in the chapter, but I use my portable band saw all the time. It is a luxury tool when you are starting out, but once you have one you'll wonder how you got on without it.

have the need for a larger GMAW machine, it is better to save a little on this apparatus to save money down the road for a more versatile GTAW machine. Generally speaking, the GTAW (Tig) machine will produce cleaner more proficient welds, on a wider range of metals than GMAW. Keep in mind that if you want to work with aluminum, the GMAW is not the best route. Even though you can get a spool gun that will work with your GMAW welder, I've never had a whole

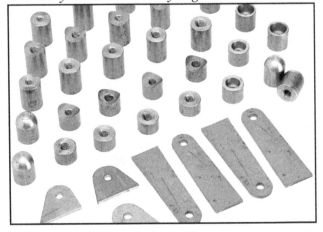

Lowbrow Customs sells this builders bung kit. It will save you tons of time during your build to have some of these around for mounting accessories.

I like the maneuverability of lifts like these. I use them far more than the platform lift I have.

My bench grinder gets more use as a buffer than anything else. I generally use hand-held grinders for any serious metal removal.

Clamps, clamps, clamps. You can never have enough of them in your shop. You'll need them to fabricate most of your parts- it's a second set of hands!

lot of luck with them. It was easier to invest in GTAW than it was trying to get the spool gun to perform effectively. If you don't have the money though, you can use the combination of GMAW and Oxy-fuel to cover most any type of welding you will ever have to do. One word of advice here related to welding with GMAW - buy a quality welding helmet. Actually, that is the case with either GTAW or GMAW. I actually use a helmet from 3M that has worked flawlessly for the time that I've had it. I started with the basic flip-type lens when I first started welding. Through time, I decided to upgrade to the auto-darkening style helmet and went with the Speedglass product. It works great, and allows me to focus more on welding than constantly raising and lowering the helmet.

I recommend an air compressor as soon as you can afford it. When I first started building motorcycles, I used mostly electric and hand tools. Even though I was able to work, nothing was fast or efficient. I started out with a fairly small 30-gallon air compressor when I could afford it. It ran almost constantly when I would get into a sanding or painting project. Beyond that, the thing was deafening, as it didn't have any sort of insulation to keep the compressor noise down. It was great for limited use, but when a project started to get really involved, it couldn't keep up. I eventually upgraded, and the higher capacity machine made my life much easier. Keep in mind when you upgrade to a large compressor that you'll need to attach it to the floor. Larger commercial compressors need to be level on the floor and attached with bolts into the concrete. I suppose that you could create a sort of wooden sled or pallet to be able to move the compressor, but I'd recommend against it because most industrial compressors stand tall and are very top heavy.

The variety of pneumatic tools available is endless, and given their construction (and with the proper care), they can outlast many electric tools. There are some electric tools that I prefer over their pneumatic counterparts. For instance, even though I do have a few pneumatic grinders, I prefer the flexibility and speed of wheel changing of

You won't just be working with metal. I use wood to layout designs, and to support projects at proper heights as I'm mocking up.

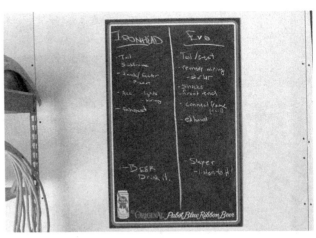

My chalkboard. Excuse the poor handwriting, but I use it all the time for drawing ideas, and listing parts of a project that need to be addressed.

If you don't have these, you aren't going to be able to make much progress. Make sure you always have a service manual at the ready.

the electric version. And because of my woodworking experience, I have a preference to battery-operated drills for their torque and portability. Generally speaking, pneumatic tools are cost-effective, and with the proper set up in your shop, they can be very convenient as well. I have a couple of different air lines running through my shop with retractable hoses that reach every inch of space including quite a distance out into the driveway for those rare months in Minnesota when it is actually nice enough to work outside (or when I decide to work on something with four wheels instead of two)!

One of my favorite small tools. I love the look of safety-wired parts. It's the small details that matter!

Just a small collection of the bungs, nuts, bolts, and tabs I have. I keep the most frequently used pieces in small containers so that I can move from project to project without having to run back to my cabinet.

I have a very simple hose-reel for use in my shop. If I need more length or multiple lines, I have hoses and connectors at the ready.

This small, portable sandblaster can handle the smaller projects, but I usually send larger parts out to be professionally blasted.

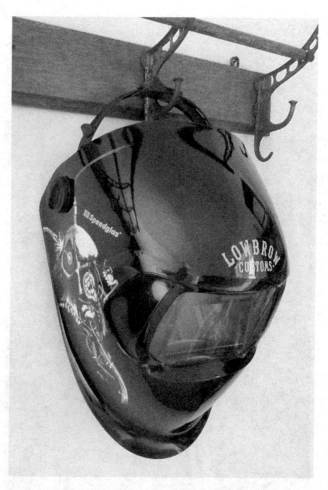

Get yourself a good auto-dimming welding helmet. It'll save your eyes, and makes things much easier when you aren't flipping your lid up and down all the time.

I use my portable band saw an incredible amount these days. Even though they tend to be a little more cumbersome than other options, the number of uses for one of these is amazing. Only limited by the thickness of the material you are putting in the throat of the saw, and the depth it will cut said material, you can get through just about anything with a band saw. As you've seen in various chapters, I use my band saw almost as much as I use the cutting wheels on my grinder. In a lot of cases, I reach for the band saw first. For instance, when it came to cutting off the frame section on the café project, it would have been just as easy to use a cutting wheel, but I preferred the saw for its control. Also, the band saw doesn't produce sparks when cutting metal. This comes in handy when I am working in the smaller area of my shop where I don't want to send a whole lot of mess flying around. It is also great when it comes to tubing, because it leaves a nice clean edge that doesn't remove any more material than the thickness of the saw blade. Its great for working on exhausts because you can cut and then tack right there on the side of the motorcycle, rather than having to go back and forth. The only complaint I do have, is that I haven't built some sort of jig to hold the saw when I want to cut things without actually holding the trigger in the "on" position. It's on my to-do list to figure something like that out down the road! My particular model of band saw was a really great deal, and actually came with a free grinder when I bought it. I see them come with free blades or accessories all the time, so watch for a good deal and snap one up when you can.

There are some other tools that receive a great deal of use in my shop depending on the project. These are the various measurement tools from rulers and dial calipers, to angle finders and torque measurement devices. When working with metal, these become extremely valuable tools to reduce waste. There are not many things as deflating as spending a large chunk of time working on a part for a motorcycle only to find out that said part doesn't fit due to improper measurement. Even on the two projects built in this book, I came upon situations where I thought I'd measured properly only to find that I had miscalculated and was forced to modify something I'd already built. That can be fine when its something minor like the

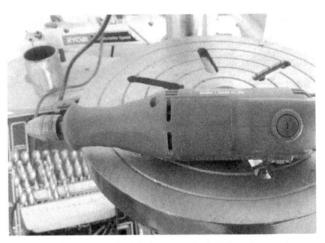

A small rotary tool will be very helpful in your shop. It can reach places no other tool can.

This little device will help your air tools last much longer. It filters out some of the water that forms in the compression process. If you are planning on painting, you'll need drier air than this provides. I have a dryer on the gun side of the process as well when I paint.

I've got drawers full of rotary tool attachments and bits that I've picked up along the way.

Buy yourself some good gaskets if you delve into rebuilding your motor. And its usually cheaper to buy the whole set rather than a few gaskets at a time.

If you have an Ironhead, you should get this DVD. It contains tons of useful information for keeping your Ironhead on the road.

length of a bolt, but can cause serious issues when it's something like building a battery box on an Ironhead only to find out that the chain doesn't clear it! The old adage of "measure twice, cut once" is as true today as it was in the past.

As much as I free form parts of builds with things like battery boxes, or exhausts - the actual mounting of these parts requires a good degree of measuring to do correctly. From a safety standpoint, I use these tools to align my wheels and chain, along with any other parts that require close tolerances to perform properly. When you start to take steps into internal engine modifications, careful measurements are required to prevent failure of parts due to incorrect alignment, improper runout, or torque that's not up to spec. Keep an eye out for deals on measuring devices. These are standardized tools that can perform well at most price points. I see coupons all the time for metal rulers and angle finders from discount tool supplies. Torque wrenches and dial calipers can be a little more tricky to find good deals on, as features and materials influence price. A beam type torque wrench is going to be less expensive than a dial type wrench. Just as a dial face caliper is going to differ in price from a digital device. All can be accurate and useful tools, it just depends on your budget and preferences to decide what is going to work best for you. I can't stress enough that proper measurement is the key to keeping your motorcycle running effectively.

When it comes to a comfortable shop, you have to do what you can with what you have. I've seen guys who build out of second-story apartments, sheds in the back yard, or under a tree out in a parking lot. The space I have is large enough to be set up by sub-area: welding, electrical, machining/fabrication, assembly, and storage. I have a small back room that I can work out of when the weather gets really cold. I can also close that area off with plastic if I need to paint or sandblast. The reality of it is that it's pretty much a two-car garage with a spare room. In a lot of ways it becomes too big of a space when tools start getting placed in one area or another. During the two builds for this book, I spent a lot of time running around looking for the right wrench or socket I've actually seen some shops that are "one project at a time" operations that are very efficient single car garages with well placed storage that would be a far better use of space than my current shop. I'm lucky to have the room, but it doesn't force me to be as neat and efficiency-minded as I should be.

Most of the time I use the standard hydraulic motorcycle lift you'd see at a tool supply. I like having both wheels free when I work, and rarely have a problem with strapping down a project to that style of lift. I do have a platform that I built years ago, but it doesn't see a whole lot of use with the exception of wiring time and assembly. I like to be able to roll the lifts and motorcycles around quite a bit to different areas of my shop, and I've just come to prefer the compact lifts. I'd imagine at some point through age, my opinion on my lift preference will change, but at this point I am still willing and able to sit on a shop floor if I have to!

Beyond that, you need to collect tools for your builds wherever and whenever you can. With a serious motorcycle addiction, you begin to realize that you will also acquire a tool acquisition addiction. Automotive bodywork hammers and dollies help you form metal for fenders and tanks. Woodworking tools help you build wooden bucks to model or form parts. Detail pieces like jockey shift knobs, hand grips or even seats can be made from wood. Even things like hobby and craft tools can be used to help move a project along. Miniature rotary tools have endless uses, from sanding hard to reach areas to clearancing moving parts that are unreachable by a full-size die grinder. A foam hot knife and a handsaw can be used to create molds for fiberglass work. Hell, I've even used kitchen tools to remove gaskets from engine surfaces when marring was a concern! The only limit to the number of tools that can be used for a motorcycle build is your imagination. So get out there and start collecting some useful tools.

Hopefully this chapter gave less experienced builders a better idea of the type of tools they are going to need to start creating their own projects.

When I'm not in my shop, this is my "office". If I need an answer or inspiration, this is where I head.

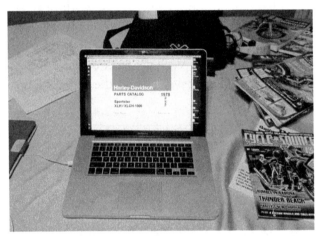

Your computer can be one of your most important tools. I have most of my manuals saved on here as .pdf files.

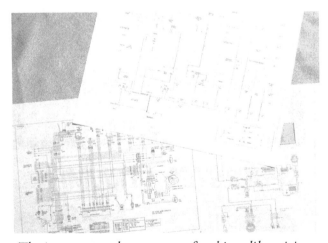

The internet can be a resource for things like wiring diagrams. I like being able to print these out so that I can mark the things I'll be using or not.

Chapter Nine

Working The Web

Your Second Set Of Tools

I know a lot of the motorcycle customization books on the market have a section on the tools necessary to complete a build. I agree that you will need basic hand tools, some sort of welding apparatus, metal-forming tools, and a comfortable place to work, in order to build a road-worthy custom motorcycle. We'll get back to those things a little later. These days, beyond the actual tools necessary for the build, the Internet is the most useful resource you will find to complete your project.

When I first started building motorcycles, there wasn't a whole lot of information available beyond parts catalogs, service manuals specific to a model, and magazines. The reality of it is that this was just a few years back - I haven't been in this

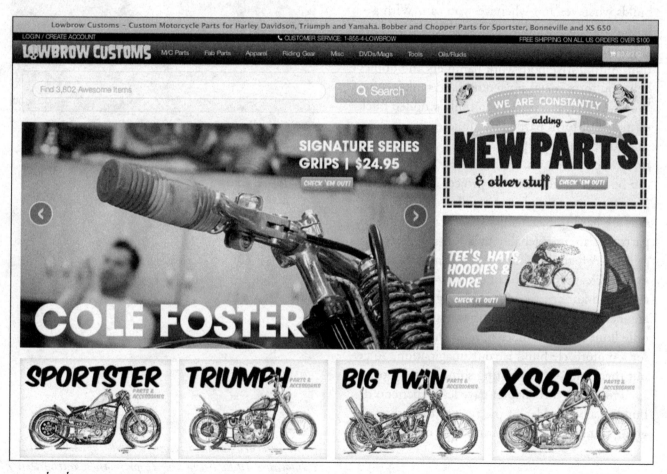

www.lowbrowcustoms.com

132

business all that long. In the last handful of years however, the amount of information available online has really blown up. The websites available to aspiring builders these days are endless. I often visit sites to ask questions that I might not readily have an answer to, to connect with other builders, or to purchase parts for a current project.

Sites like Chop Cult (chopcult.com), The Jockey Journal (jockeyjournal.com), and XL Forum (xlforum.net) provide moderated information by people located around the world. Many of the members of these sites are long time motorcycle mechanics, some who have specialized in Harley-Davidson motorcycles. Those that might not be certified mechanics are often engineers, or machinists, or craftsman that have spent much of their lives building and maintaining motorcycles with whatever free time they have. Most are more than willing to give their insight on any problem a home-builder might encounter. But just like anywhere, there are rules to be followed when using these sites. Even though most of the people who frequent these forums would agree that "there are no stupid questions," I would ask that you at least check your service manual (the one I know you already purchased) before throwing a question out to the masses. The sites are also usually

broken down pretty well by topic, so a search might bring answers even quicker than actually posting a question that might have been answered more than once already. Don't assume you are the

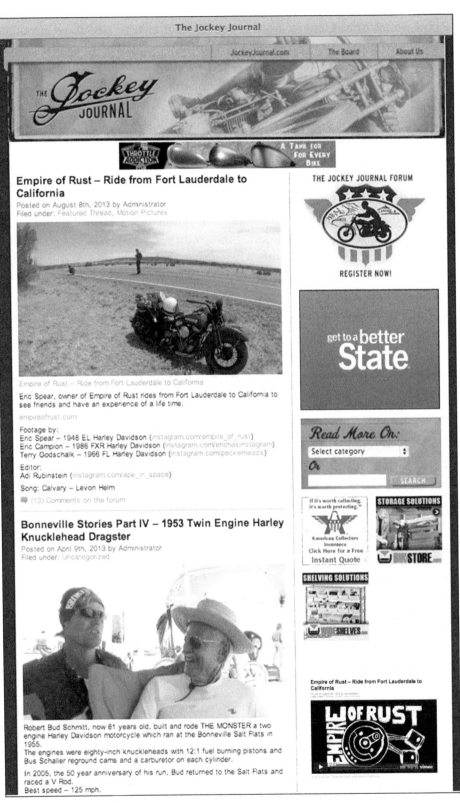

www.jockeyjournal.com

first person that's ever had the problem you are having. Search some keywords and see where that takes you first. Be aware however, that sometimes you are going to get an answer that is completely incorrect. Give a question you post a little time before you act on it. I once posted a question after searching tirelessly in my manual and all of my other resources. I received an answer fairly quickly and figured that because the response came quickly, and seemed fairly logical, that they'd figured out the solution to my problem. Unfortunately for me, I made the repair as stated by the person who posted on my question only to come to find that it actually made my issues worse. A couple days later, I checked back in the forum on my posting to find another poster had refuted the first poster's response with the correct solution. I repaired the issue, but also had to fix the other issues that arose after my first fix. I would look at questions you post in builder forums much the same way as seeking out a medical cure. It might be better to get a second opinion before you make a decision on what action you really need to take.

Also, it is always a good idea to stay positive when interacting within these sites. I've seen plenty of projects that I thought were aesthetic nightmares, or that just didn't suit my tastes. Its best to just move on quietly when seeing things like that, because the person building it might be a wealth of knowledge you might need. Everybody has his or her own style, and even though you might not like it, it is better not to voice your opinion.

I guess I look at interacting in the forums much like I do when interacting in public. I think a lot of people tend to forget their place when they make a comment online, because they figure that they'll never see the person they are commenting to in person. So what difference does it make, right? I like to look at every online interaction as if it was happening in person (you never know when it might). If I'm at a motorcycle show and I don't like a specific build, I keep walking. I'm not going to stand there and call out the builder. Its too small of a world these days to get negative online or otherwise. Nothing will get you banned from a site (or life for that matter) quicker than being an asshole.

Beyond providing a place for questions and answers, these sites provide a place for enthusiasts to build brotherhood with other builders. The great thing about the Internet is that it brought all of us closer together in a sense. I can log on to one of these

www.sportyspecialties.com

sites, and talk to a person that I may have met on the other side of the country at some rally or event. I can also throw the feelers out there to see who is doing what I'm doing in the same neighborhood. It can be especially helpful to figure out who is nearby when you have a problem you just can't fix. Every builder is going to have one of those moments where they throw up their hands, exasperated. With these forums, a case of beer can become currency when it comes to a fresh set of eyes on a project. Many times I've checked to see who is nearby that can help me out with a project issue. In a lot of cases it is to borrow tools or abilities I might not necessarily possess in trade for some expertise or tool I might have. Often times these relationships are what companies are born from.

Most of us don't just build bikes to build bikes. We hit the open road as much as we can.

Breakdowns happen, and those of us that ride older iron know very well that there aren't a lot of shops out there, let alone are they open on weekends when most of us are cruising. When I'm out riding, I go out of my way to go places I haven't been before. Because of that, I often don't know the area I'm riding into very well in terms of resources. I'm not much of one for planning when I take off, so I usually depend on my smart phone to keep me out of trouble when my tool roll fails me. One of the great things available to us these days on many of the enthusiast websites is a spreadsheet of people who submitted their names as willing to help their brothers if a breakdown happens in their vicinity. On some of the sites, these good Samaritans even list equipment they have available to help out. Its good to know in advance if somebody has a truck or welder or some other machine available in case of a cata-

www.lickscycles.com

strophic event. Luckily these days there aren't too many roads where you can't get cellular reception, so this method of finding help can be a lot more effective (and safe) than knocking on a random farmer's door. I try to make myself available to bikers near my shop and near my home, just as I hope they would for me. It's all part of being a motorcycle enthusiast.

Because many of us have limited access to swap meets (they're becoming a rare breed these days), we have to utilize the Internet in creative ways to get the parts we need. Of course there are the many big box online retailers available to us, but most of the forum sites also have sections where parts/projects are accessible for purchase. I spend a lot of time in the for sale section of many sites. Because many of the parts I buy are for motorcycles for which there aren't many outlets for new parts, I have to check back frequently to see if something I need is going to pop up. Also, because of the fluctuation of price in motorcycles from region to region, it is often a good idea to watch these sites for a model that may come up for a steal. That becomes especially important for those of us who live in an area where motorcycles sell for a premium because the seasons are short or

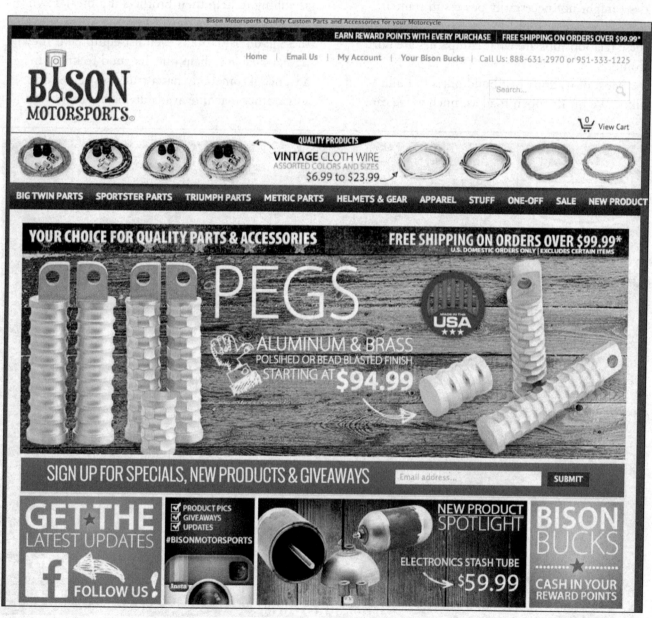

www.bisonmotorsports.com

136

the quantities are limited. A used Sportster in the South is generally going to go for quite a bit less than it would in the Midwest. Sometimes the price differential is so drastic that it might be worth the time and the gas money to take a road trip down to pick up a new project or basket-case of parts. Don't have a truck? Remember what I was just telling you about building relationships with the guys you find in your area? Hopefully, if they do come along they can help keep you from making a quick decision on something just because you drove a few miles. Don't let the fact that you drove a long distance influence your decision when you go to check out a potential project. More than once I've gone to look at a project motorcycle some distance away and thought, "I don't have anything else lined up at this price, I'm going to have to jump on this even though it isn't what was advertised." If you think about that in the long run, the gas you spent checking out a project and walking away can be far less than the money you might spend if you sign on for a project where you get in over your head.

When it comes to parts for sale on the online forums, I often see very interesting historic parts posted that a builder would not have had access to unless they physically saw them hanging in the neighborhood shop. From old molded tanks, to complete digger frames, to rare racing memorabilia, I've seen it all posted in

the online for sale sections. These days, I'm seeing a lot more of those parts online then I am at swap meets. Early on, I thought that the slow death of swap meets was a terrible thing. I love digging through old milk crates filled with greasy used parts. The hunt for something that nobody else had seen was always in my head. Unfortunately, those finds got fewer and fewer as time went on at the swap meets I was attending. It wasn't that the parts had all been bought up and put back on the road. More likely it was that the more savvy swap meet sellers realized that the internet was a far more valuable marketplace than the local county fairgrounds. It seems like swap meets have become the last ditch effort to get rid of take-off parts that

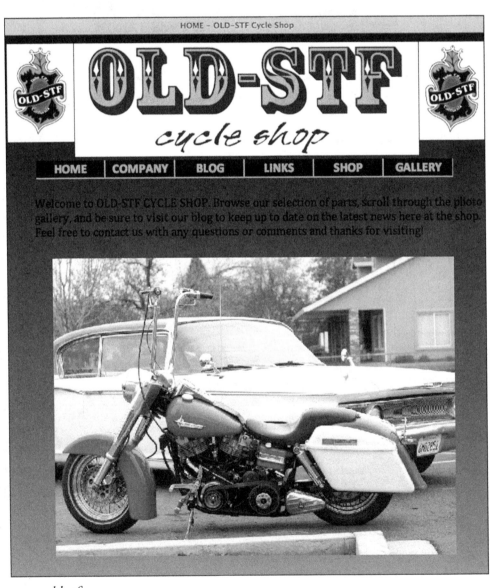

www.old-stf.com

137

couldn't be sold anywhere else. I look at some tables at the few remaining swap meets I still attend locally and wonder why they just don't take the parts in for scrap money rather than waste time trying to sell things nobody wants. Its getting harder and harder to find a diamond in the rough. All is not lost however, there are a few really good swap meets left in the country. You guys in California are pretty lucky when it comes to weekly swap meets with a large variety of quality parts.

Other areas of the country, especially those with snow, tend to have to look a little harder for good stuff. Luckily, the Internet has become our swap meet, and we are better for it.

Along with used parts, a lot of guys are selling custom parts they make in small or one-off quantities. I don't have a lathe or a mill in my personal shop. I know how to use them, and have access offsite when I need it, but in many cases, I leave things like foot pegs and handgrips up to guys who are sitting in their shop at their lathe doing a dozen or so at a time. I will hop behind the lathe for a spacer or something mechanically crucial, but creatively, I tend to lean towards more caveman-esque fire and hammer projects. Most of these guys are using their machine tools every single day, so fabrication of certain parts becomes second nature to them.

Often, I see builders on the enthusiast sites produce something for their personal project where they ask the opinion of the masses as to whether they would buy a particular part if they produced a few of them for other members. If the opinion of the group is positive, the person builds more to satisfy the demand of the forum.

www.jpcycles.com

Thus, it becomes a place for creative builders to create products that might not otherwise see the open market. Plus, because they are producing certain accessories on a daily basis, they can whip out a part faster than somebody that does not have the proper tools. So if you are planning to buy a part for your build, do yourself a favor and check the classified section of some of the web forums for something that might suit your needs. Most of the time the part will be better quality than many of the mass-produced parts out there. And often, the part will be cheaper than anything you can find at the big box retailers because an aspiring builder is just trying to get their name out there.

I don't want to completely alienate the big-box motorcycle parts retailers in this chapter. I will admit that I still use them on a semi-regular basis. Mainly, I use them for wear parts like tires, brake pads, and fluids. Because they sell so many of these types of parts, they are able to sell them at very competitive prices. Some of them still carry a good supply of parts for older motorcycles. More of my purchases these days though are made at sites specialized for builders and customizers. As you will see throughout this book, I use lowbrowcustoms.com on a regular basis. They are an excellent online resource for the Sportster custom builder, and carry a wide range of quality parts. Also, you might try bisonmotorsports.com, oldstf.com, or oldbikebarn.com for builder parts and supplies as well. I have personally used all of these sites and recommend them for the customized parts you may want to purchase instead of fabricating your own. Another nice part of the smaller retailers is that they usually have a great tech department. Because they specialize in a smaller number of motorcycle models, they are able to answer questions more readily than some of the large retailers. Some of the smaller sites also have tech areas where they actually show step-by-step installations of some of their more popular products.

www.oldbikebarn.com

Don't forget about the many auction sites available these days! Craigslist and EBay both provide resources for the home builder. Locally speaking, I spend a lot of time on Craigslist looking for deals that can be had on motorcycles. Because the prices fluctuate so drastically here in Minnesota depending on the season, I'm a lot less likely to be checking local auction sites in the spring and summer. During the fall and winter however, I spend a bunch of time looking for projects to fill the off-season. Keep in mind that people often don't have space to store their motorcycles over the winter, so they might be a little more willing to lower their asking price versus paying storage fees.

Craigslist is also a great place to find "basket-case" motorcycles. People are constantly pulling unused motorcycles out of sheds and garages to sell online. They don't have the resources or want to get them in running condition, so they resort to the online auctions to get them off their property. When it comes to a non-running Ironhead I find online, you can bet I'm making the call to see what's what, and how much they want for it!

If you are looking for specific parts, especially used parts, I would suggest taking a look on EBay to see if you can find a deal. Some of the

140

more resourceful would-be basket-case sellers take the time and effort to disassemble parts in hopes of making more money on individual sales. This can have its positives and negatives in terms of the buyer. If you don't need a whole engine or motorcycle, or are not able to afford either - EBay gives more of an opportunity to find singular components. The downside to this is that sellers need to pay fees to use the services of an auction site, so the buyer is often paying a premium to make up for it. Because of this premium, I generally don't look for project motorcycles on EBay- especially if I plan to sell it myself after customization. With profits available on home built customs so low, the auction site premiums make it even harder to break even. However, if I am looking for a specific model for myself- or a customer, I will check to see if there is something available near me at a reasonable price.

The online sites are not just a tool for useful builder information and supply. They also provide for builder inspiration as well. As I said previously, there are literally thousands of people working on project bikes around the world. Many of these people are documenting builds as a way to share what they are learning as they go. They are building parts specific to their project, or modifying parts in interesting ways. When I'm not in the garage working on my own projects, I spend lots of time checking out what other people are doing. Mainly, I look to see what direction the trends in motorcycle design are heading. I think you should

build what you want, and what looks good to you. But I also think the greater your exposure to other builds, the more creative you can get with your own projects. You shouldn't seek to copy what somebody else has built. But rather, take the parts of the project that interested you and expand on them in your own creative way.

www.chopcult.com

141

Wolfgang Books On The Web
http://www.wolfpub.com

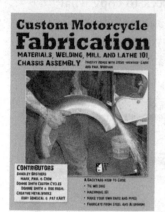

CUSTOM MOTORCYCLE FABRICATION

Owner of Bare Knuckle Choppers and long time motorcycle builder and fabricator, Paul Wideman is the perfect author for this book. With experience as both a hands-on builder and technical editor for Cycle Source Magazine, Paul has exactly the skill-set needed to write a book on fabrication.

Some commonly fabricated parts like handle bars and exhaust systems are covered as separate

topics, along with sections on building simple brackets and mounts.

Learn how professionals like Paul bypass the catalog and build their parts from scratch instead. This is an essential building book, helping you build the necessary skills needed to assemble a truly unique kick-ass motorcycle.

| Eleven Chapters | 144 Pages | $27.95 | Over 400 color images - 100% color |

CUSTOM BIKE BUILDING BASICS

Custom Bike Building Basics is the basic bible that at-home builders need to build and modify their own motorcycle.

Grass roots bikes are often built using a "donor bike" as the foundation and source for the majority of parts. Chapters Four and Five offer tips on choosing the best donor bike.

The final topics are two that we often find intimidating: Upholstery and Wiring. With one chapter on each Topic, the mystery and fear are eliminated.

This is the one book you need before you tear into that donor bike and begin the process of creating your own motorcycle.

| Nine Chapters | 144 Pages | $27.95 | Over 400 photos, 100% color |

KOSMOSKI'S NEW KUSTOM PAINTING SECRETS

Jon Kosmoski - the King of Kustom Painters - puts over four decades of experience into Kosmoski's New Kustom Painting Secrets. No how-to-paint would be complete without at least two, start-to-finish paint jobs. Kosmoski's New Kustom Painting Secrets contains both a hot rod and a motorcycle paint job. The sequences start at the very beginning with the metal preparation, and

moves through all the primer and filler stages necessary to make the panels perfect, before any top-coat can be applied. The paint jobs include artwork and flames, application of the candy paint, and the final clearcoats. Kosmoski's New Kustom Painting Secrets uses over 400 color images and 144 pages to explain a lifetime's worth of custom painting experience.

| Eight Chapters | 144 Pages | $27.95 | Over 400 photos, 100% color |

TATTOO LETTERING BIBLE

This, the newest in a long list of Tattoo Bibles from Superior Tattoo, gives both tattoo artists and tattoo aficionados 128 pages of tattoo fonts, alphabets and banners. At Superior we've produced a variety of compact books on lettering styles over the years, and each of our small lettering manuals has been very well received. To date, thousands of those have been purchased or downloaded as ebooks. But why flip through several books to find

the perfect font?

If you, or your customer, wants his or her loved one's name on a memorial, there is only one book you will need to pull off the shelf. Day in and day out, this book will be utilized. You won't find a better assortment of lettering than what you find in Tattoo Lettering Bible. Be sure this one is part of your collection!

| 128 Pages | $27.95 | 100% color |

142

Wolfgang Publication Titles
For a current list visit our website at www.wolfpub.com

ILLUSTRATED HISTORY
Ultimate Triumph Collection	$49.95
American Police Motorcycles - Revised	$24.95

BIKER BASICS
Custom Motorcycle Fabrication	$27.95
Custom Bike Building Basics	$24.95
Custom Bike Building Advanced	$24.95
Sportster/Buell Engine Hop-Up Guide	$24.95
Sheet Metal Fabrication Basics	$24.95
How to Fix American T-Twin Motorcycles	$27.95

COMPOSITE GARAGE
Composite Materials Handbook #1	$27.95
Composite Materials Handbook #2	$27.95
Composite Materials Handbook #3	$27.95

HOT ROD BASICS
How to A/C Your Hot Rod	$24.95
So-Cal Speed Shop's How to Build Hot Rod Chassis	$24.95
Hot Rod Wiring	$27.95
How to Chop Tops	$24.95

CUSTOM BUILDER SERIES
How to Build A Café Racer	$27.95
Advanced Custom Motorcycle Wiring - Revised	$27.95
How to Build an Old Skool Bobber Sec Ed	$27.95
How To Build The Ultimate V-Twin Motorcycle	$24.95
Advanced Custom Motorcycle Assembly & Fabrication	$27.95
How to Build a Cheap Chopper	$27.95

LIFESTYLE
Bean're — Motorcycle Nomad	$18.95
George The Painter	$18.95
The Colorful World of Tattoo Models	$34.95

MOTORCYCLE RESTORATION SERIES
Triumph Restoration - Unit 650cc	$29.95
Triumph MC Restoration Pre-Unit	$29.95

SHEET METAL
Advanced Sheet Metal Fabrication	$27.95
Ultimate Sheet Metal Fabrication	$24.95
Sheet Metal Bible	$29.95

AIR SKOOL SKILLS
How To Draw Monsters	$27.95
Airbrush Bible	$29.95
How Airbrushes Work	$24.95

PAINT EXPERT
How To Airbrush, Pinstripe & Goldleaf	$27.95
Kosmoski's New Kustom Painting Secrets	$27.95
Pro Pinstripe Techniques	$27.95
Advanced Pinstripe Art	$27.95

TATTOO U Series
Advanced Tattoo Art - Revised	$27.95
Cultura Tattoo Sketchbook	$32.95
Tattoo Sketchbook by Jim Watson	$32.95
Tattoo Sketchbook by Nate Powers	$27.95
Into The Skin The Ultimate Tattoo Sourcebook (Includes companion DVD)	$34.95
American Tattoos	$27.95
Tattoo Bible Book One	$27.95
Tattoo Bible Book Two	$27.95
Tattoo Bible Book Three	$27.95
Tattoo Lettering Bible	$27.95

TRADE SCHOOL SERIES
Learning The English Wheel	$27.95

GUIDE BOOKS
Honda Motorcycles - Enthusiast Guide	$27.95

Sources

3M http://www.3m.com/

7MetalWest http://7metalwest.com/

AirTech Streamlining http://www.airtech-streamlining.com/

Avon Grips http://avongrips.com/shop/

Bench Mark http://benchmark.bigcartel.com/

Benjie's Café Racers http://www.benjiescaferacer.com/

Biltwell Inc. http://www.biltwellinc.com/

Burly Brand http://www.burlybrand.com/

Cycle Electric http://www.cycleelectricinc.com/

Cycle Standard available at lowbrowcustoms.com

David Bird available at lowbrowcustoms.com

Discount Steel Inc. http://www.discountsteel.com/

Fab Kevin http://www.fabkevin.com/

Front St Cycle http://frontstcycle.blogspot.com/

The Gasbox http://www.thegasbox.com/index.html

Goodridge http://www.goodridge.net/

Hammer Performance http://hammerperf.com/

Hobart Welders http://www.hobartwelders.com/

LC Fabrications http://www.lcfabrications.com/

Led Sled Customs http://www.ledsledcustoms.com/

Lowbrow Customs http://www.lowbrowcustoms.com/

Mikuni http://www.mikuni.com/

Minneapolis Oxygen Company http://www.mplso2.com/

Mooneyes http://www.mooneyesusa.com/

NRHS Performance http://www.nrhsperformance.com/

Performance Machine http://www.performancemachine.com/

Pro-Custom Powder Coating
http://www.procustompowdercoating.com/

Roland Sands Design http://www.rolandsands.com/

Ryca Motors http://www.rycamotors.com/

S&S http://www.sscycle.com/

Special79 http://specialseventynine.blogspot.com/

Storz Performance http://www.storzperf.com/

TC Bros Choppers http://www.tcbroschoppers.com/

The Speed Merchant http://thespeedmerchant.net/

Zippers Performance http://www.zippersperformance.com/